PRAISES FOR "Spiritual Happy Hour"

In this often hilarious yet profound book, Jen and Janelle recount their inspired partnership, their wild adventures, and their incredible spiritual awakenings and creations as they share "spirits" and all things of the spirit for us all to enjoy. This is a gorgeous read for anyone searching for meaning and freedom in their life. I loved it.

Sonia Choquette
New York Times bestselling author of *The Answer is Simple*

In *Spiritual Happy Hour*—**A DOUBLE SHOT OF B.A.D.**, Janelle Hoyland and Jennifer Louziotis invite us into the Absolute Good interpenetrating the Universe that mothers us, that tenderly caresses and guides each and every one of us through our inherent intuitive capacity.

Michael Bernard Beckwith
Author of *Life Visioning* and *Spiritual Liberation*
www.agapelive.com

Jen recounts the compelling story about her and Janelle's inspired partnership, which led to adventures and awakenings beyond perhaps what either had imagined. It's liberating to hear a real life account about ways the universe orchestrates magical happenings. Their trust in this infinite wisdom allowed them to create something greater than themselves, extending ripples of goodness to their listeners and in ways that they may never fully realize. By fueling the spark in each other and in themselves, they profoundly fuel the spark in others.

Karen L. Garvey, MBA
Speaker, Author, Intuitive, Personal & Professional Coach

Wow! It took me a bit to get started. And when I did I couldn't put my phone down. It's almost weird the way I connected to it more now than ever before. I was brought up in a way to believe in a super power and I always did. Before anything good had to happen, whether it was as simple as a travel plan or a board exam for dental school or even a birthday, we would be trained to pray to God to thank him and ask him to make things go smooth. And I did it without putting too much thought into it. So I wasn't as spiritually connected as Jen was growing up, but I did it as a way of growing up.

But as I got older and life became more complicated and more responsibilities came my way, I was hit with a thunderstorm and my dad passed suddenly. It seemed like it came at an inopportune time (but maybe no time is opportune) and I felt like I lost faith in everything and in a super power. But reading Jennifer Louziotis and Janelle Hoyland's book made me feel that it is important to have some belief because it helped me move on and to remember that things happen for a reason, and to be sad about life and live in a feeling that things are unfair only affects the person who is going through it. To be able to move on and to live each day in a peaceful way, one has to believe in a spiritual power and know that there is someone watching over you and if you believe in that, things do get better. So this book is a must read and I definitely recommend it. Personally it has helped me a lot.

Dr. Sonia Kholi, DDS

Tune In

Spiritual Happy Hour

A DOUBLE SHOT OF B.A.D.—
Being, Allowing, Doing

By
Rev. Janelle Hoyland, PH.D.
and
Jennifer Louziotis

Houston, Texas

PUBLISHER'S NOTE:

This book is a work of fiction. People, places, events, and situations are the product of the author's imagination. Any resemblance to actual persons, living or dead, or historical events, is purely coincidental.

ISBN-13: 978-0-9981980-0-2 (Paperback)
978-0-9981980-1-9 (Ebook)
First Edition

Library of Congress Control Number: TBD

Houston, Texas
Produced in the United States of America
10 9 8 7 6 5 4 3 2 1

DEDICATION

To the Sandy Hook families. We started our journey on December 14th 2012, the day of the Sandy Hook School shooting, which happened 10 minutes prior to us going live on the air. We decided to do the photos for the cover in honor of those families who lost their children. We took the photos on the beach in Sea Bright, New Jersey on one of the playgrounds built by the Sandy Ground Project: Where Angels Play. This playground was built in memory of Anne Marie Murphy, special education teacher. We wanted to keep the memory of those playful angels up in heaven.

ACKNOWLEDGEMENTS BY JEN

So many people came together to offer me support and guidance during the writing of this book and their insight, enthusiasm, and hard work behind the scenes helped to make this book a success. I am forever grateful.

Manon Lavoie and Aimee Ravichandran, thank you for all your hard work and support.

Parisa Moayedi, thank you so much for creating the beautiful cover design for the book. I am so grateful.

Stephen, Karen, Anne, Jon and Jill, the writing of this book would not have been possible without your support. Thanks so much for being part of my life and for listening to me when I need someone to lean on and for giving me encouragement throughout my life.

Mom and Dad, thank you for your unwavering love and support and for constantly teaching me to follow my dreams and to just be who I am. And for the endless phone calls when I was living in NYC, NJ, Tokyo, and back to NJ.

Janelle Hoyland, thank you so much for being part of my journey this time around, for being so vulnerable and open, and for always saying yes to life, no matter what is in front of you or what is in your way. Just like with Dee and the kids, I don't have words to describe how much your friendship means to me. Your unconditional love, support, and belief in me has change my being and my life. I am not the same person I was in Hawaii, and our friendship has played a major role in that transformation. I am forever grateful. Thanks for the long talks at my kitchen table and in your office and over the phone and for the laughter, tears of joy, and adventures we've shared together. Your living life full out helps me remember who I really am.

Finally, Dee, Sophia and Matthew, words really can't describe how grateful I am to have you in my life. Thank you for your unconditional love and support throughout the creation of the show and the writing of this book and really every day we share together as a family. Dee, for believing in me even when I wasn't sure that I believed in myself. You are such a gift in my life.

SPECIAL GRATITUDE BY JANELLE

I am so beyond moved by this whole journey. I have so many people to show gratitude to.

Most of all my hubby, Steve, of 22 years. I love you honey for every ounce of support you give me. I am completely blown away by my kids Kelci, Zoie and 3 my son for constantly rallying behind me. You believed in me before anyone else. You never let me forget why I do everything I do.

My sister. I could never ask for a better best friend then you.

My parents, who listened to me since high school say I know what I am going to do. I love you.

Jennifer Louziotis, I am at a complete loss of adequate words for who you are in my life. You have pushed me and cried with me. Thanks for hanging in with me. Without you this book would not have happened.

Parisa Moayedi, thank you for beautifully designing a masterful cover. Your friendship is such a gift in my life. My life would be incomplete without you.

Kim, you are a light in this world and a light in my life. It's an honor to share in this journey with you.

I am also moved by Sonia Choquette and Michael Beckwith, the ground breakers that set the stage before us. You have both allowed me to understand myself to a greater degree.

Our behind the scenes crew: Aimee, for getting my vision about what this book needed to feel like. You are awesome. Manon, your attention to detail in this book is a true gift. Thank you for the late nights. I know you love them.

To all the loving souls that have allowed me to help them change their lives, this is for you. I am so beyond grateful to get to serve in this way for all of you.

I am grateful to my Team of guides, angels and God for allowing me to come back and do this again.

TABLE OF CONTENT

PREFACE

The vision for this book was born out of a phone call that took place between myself and Janelle Hoyland in March of 2010. That phone call was actually an answer to a long-forgotten prayer that I'd put out to God thirteen years earlier while I was living in New York City as a graduate student. It would take me three years after that call to appreciate the full significance of my friendship with Janelle; the spiritual magnitude of our talks about life, and to understand that the radio show we were called to create together were all pieces of the answer to that long lost prayer, and to questions I had been asking my whole life. Not once in that three-year period did it dawn on me that God *had* been listening back in 1997, and not only had he listened, but he brought me *exactly* what life had caused me to ask for, and a lot more.

For me, this book is a story about partnership, connection and blind faith. I was born a twin and, as a result of the relationship between my brother and me, I thought I had a solid understanding of what it meant to be in a partnership and share a special connection with another person. As I moved through life, I tried to recreate the same close bond Jon and I shared from birth in every other partnership I formed. I did this by looking outside of myself and focusing my attention on the other person's needs, but my partnerships never reached that same level of closeness or fun that I experienced with my twin. I wanted to understand what was missing and what I needed to do differently to experience that connection.

The answer unfolded as a direct result of my partnership with Janelle Hoyland during the radio show called *"Spiritual Happy Hour"* that we began co-hosting in 2012. Over time, Janelle got me to see that instead of searching *outside* myself to find connection, I needed to turn inward and form a partnership with my Divine Self first. That Divine partnership would serve as a solid foundation for me and would guide me in all other partnerships I formed. Here's how this story started for me...

For as long as I can remember, I've always had a longing to find out why I was put on Earth and what I was here to do, not in a small sense but in a much larger sense. I was trying to find out who I was in relation to the Universe. And it wasn't just me I wondered about. I questioned why everyone was here. This longing wasn't something I learned from anyone in my family; it came from within me—it was part of me and somehow I knew it was connected to God.

Starting at around the age of five, I experienced this longing as a nervous feeling in the pit of my stomach. It was a combination between a nudge and a feeling of agitation. I didn't understand what the feeling was, and I couldn't make it go away. I enjoyed life like every other kid—playing and having fun with my brothers and sister—but I always had an awareness of that underlying feeling and because of it I started to try to pay attention more closely to the world around me. There were two instances from my childhood that I feel were connected to this awareness. The first was when I was six years old. I was raised in the Catholic Church and I had started to learn about who God and the Angels were and what Heaven was and I remember wondering if they lived in the sky why were we living on Earth.

At the same time, I became very interested in a religious cartoon called *Davey and Goliath* about a young boy and his dog. In each episode, Davey would come up against a problem in life and, in order to solve the problem, he would have to put his faith in God. The show made an impression on me because Davey could hear God speaking to him, and I wondered why he could hear God but I couldn't. I remember thinking that somehow what Davey was doing in this cartoon was related to that feeling in my stomach. It felt like I had discovered a single missing piece to a much larger puzzle.

The second event that stands out in my mind from childhood happened when I turned ten. Our family got cable TV and HBO ran a special series on the life and predictions of Nostradamus. I watched that special over and over again because it depicted an actual person who has the ability to communicate to God—not just a cartoon character. Up until that time, I had never heard the word "psychic." I had no idea (other than from *Davey and Goliath*) that it was possible for people to communicate with Heaven and to predict the future. I thought if I could learn to communicate the same way Nostradamus did, then I could finally start to figure out the answer to that nagging feeling I had. I also wondered, again, why some people had the ability to predict the future but others could not.

So I became drawn to psychics, but I wasn't born into a family that had any clue about or interest in that topic. No one talked about psychics or intuition or spirituality in the 1970s and 1980s in my family so I kept this interest mostly to myself. I tried to look for more information about how to be psychic in books and TV shows. This went on from the time I was ten until I graduated high school.

There were times during this part of my life when I knew that my questions about who I was in relation to God or the Universe were very different from what other kids my age thought about. Sometimes I wanted to fit in more with other kids instead of questioning life: I wished I could be good at sports and not think so intensely about what we were all here to do, but every time I tried to ignore this longing in me and forget about all my questions, the longing would only get stronger. So for the most part I lived my life like everyone else; going to school, socializing with friends, and eventually getting a job, but I always had that feeling in the pit of my stomach and a need to find an answer to my deeper questions about life.

By the time I entered my twenties, topics like spirituality and intuition were becoming more mainstream and there had been many books written that focused on connecting to and relaying messages from loved ones on the other side. One author that really stood out for me during this time was Sonia Choquette. I was drawn to her story of growing up as a third generation psychic healer in a large family that relied daily on tapping into intuition to make decisions. Sonia made learning about psychic skills and communicating with the other side seem normal. Reading her books gave me validation and a sense of belonging. Many of my friends at the time questioned why I would ever want to connect to the other side but Sonia's view was why *wouldn't* you want to connect?

Finally, I didn't feel different for thinking there was more to this world than what I could see or for wanting to understand more about the unseen world and the role that Divine guidance plays in helping us to tap into it. According to Sonia, we are *meant* to connect to that world. It is our birthright to do so. I was also drawn to Sonia's teaching style. Even though a big part of her mission was to teach people how to communicate with the other side, she was also a mother with a young family and not some cartoon character or ancient healer that I learned about when I was younger. The fact that she had real life struggles and used intuition to help her solve them was what I valued and appreciated when I read her books. I also learned more about who the players were on the other side other than God and the angels. She explained the different types of spirit guides, helpers and master teachers, and shared her knowledge about those who had helped her in her life and how we could rely on them, too, for guidance. This was exactly what I'd been looking for. I wanted to find someone who was psychic who could teach me how to hone my own psychic skills on a step-by-step basis.

Sonia was clear that everyone has the ability to tap into their sixth sense and that we should be using it every day. So I set out to learn how to connect by doing as many psychic exercises as I could find from many different psychic authors. I tried meditation, clearing my aura, setting positive intentions, clearing space, just to name a few. I did this over several months and felt like I was studying intently, but nothing really changed. I can see now that I wasn't giving any one thing enough time to work. I would try one exercise for a few weeks and when I didn't see any changes, I would get frustrated and go to another exercise or to another psychic author and start the process all over again. I was taking in the information on an intellectual level, but I had no idea how to integrate what I was learning into my life or into my being. I also didn't know what part of my approach needed to change so that I could finally make a connection.

As the weeks went by, I started to get more frustrated with God. I believed what all the psychic authors were saying: that there is a ton of Divine help available to us to use at any time to solve problems or bring joy into our lives. All the psychic authors I was reading made it sound so easy to connect and use Divine assistance, but I wasn't seeing any difference in my life. I kept thinking, "Why would God give us all these helpers and not make it super easy for all of us to connect to them?" That just seemed senseless in my mind. I wanted to be able to hear the Divine guidance loud and clear, but instead it was as if I was stuck in a bad game of Telephone. No messages were getting through on my line; it was as if my plastic telephone receiver was filled with rocks. To me, it felt like the people who were psychic had a cheat sheet for life and I wanted that, too. I wanted a roadmap to help me figure out why we were all here and to help me live a better life. I felt that I had an intimate relationship with God—meaning I didn't just leave thinking about him or talking to him to the hour of church on Sunday—so I expected some kind of help from him directly with my learning about Divine connection, but I just wasn't seeing it at all.

One day as I was reading Sonia's Choquette's book, *The Dairy of a Psychic*, I came across a paragraph in which she describes teaching small classes in her basement before she became famous. As I read this paragraph, I said to myself, "Well, there it is again… another famous psychic that started out teaching classes in the basement of someone's house." I again started to become really frustrated at God. I wanted so much to have an easy connection to the other side, but it just wasn't happening. I really wanted to be taught by someone in person. I wanted a personal teacher who could demonstrate to me how to connect to the other side, one who could answer my questions and who I could share my progress with, in person, over a period of weeks. I didn't know anyone in New York who could do that, and I couldn't move to Chicago to join Sonia's groups. Because I had recently been reading so much about the law of attraction, I thought I would challenge God to find out if he was really listening. In my mind this was a test, but it was also my last straw. I had given God years of study and effort, and now I wanted to see how much he would really give back. I kept reading over and over again that anything we wanted to achieve or attain on Earth was possible for all of us. We just had to ask.

So I thought in anger…

"Okay, God. Here goes…I'm ASKING…" Still holding on to Sonia Choquette's book, I spoke out loud. "What about me? Where's *my famous* psychic? Where's my GURU? I want classes taught in *MY* basement." (During this time I had no basement—I didn't even own a house—I was living in apartment in NYC). "I've been working so hard trying to figure out life. I've been reading so much and I'm tired. I'm tired of trying to figure this out on my own. Where's *my* person? Send me my person. *I'm ready.* I'm ready *now.* I want a Road Map." I was angry. I was having a bit of a tantrum. But I said it.

Nothing happened.

Not that I expected this magical person to appear in my apartment that afternoon (well, maybe I did) but nothing earthshattering happened, and so I went on with my life and focused on work and dating and friends and completely forgot about that prayer.

I did continue to read about spirituality, but gradually my focus turned to my job and my personal life for the next three years. I also continued to read more books written by Sonia Choquette and every now and then I would go on her website to look at seminars she was teaching in different cities. I was always drawn to her week-long workshop called Translucent You which took place annually in Hawaii. I really wanted to attend this workshop, but felt I could never afford the time off or the cost of the trip to Hawaii.

A Divine Appointment on the other side of the world

I met my husband Dee and got married in 2004, and in 2005, due to a job transfer at his company, we moved to Tokyo. Leaving our friends and family and moving six thousand miles away was a very daunting task, but we adjusted somewhat easily to expat life in Japan. We made a lot of friends our first year, and we enjoyed traveling and getting to know the country, its people and its customs. I was surprised to realize that leaving New York City and all its craziness (traffic, crowds, noise) was a relief for me. I missed my family and friends terribly but felt at home in the vibration of Tokyo. I hadn't realized how hard it was for me to truly relax in New York City. From the other side of the world, I could finally see how frazzled and rushed I had felt living and working in New York City. Despite the chaos of Tokyo, I experienced a feeling of calmness and I actually felt more centered living among thirteen million people than I did back home. I didn't read as many books about spirituality as there weren't many English bookstores, but I did start practicing yoga on a daily basis (something I tried to do in New York City many times and failed). I started to feel more open and I was really happy. Family came to visit often during that first year and our first child, Sophia, was born in 2006.

Things shifted for me in 2007 when I suffered a miscarriage. The old feeling of wanting to know more about how I fit into the world started coming back and, at the same time, I was struggling to move through grief. I scheduled a psychic reading with Sonia by phone to get some answers regarding my future. I hoped I could boost my spirits by taking a brief look at what was coming up for me. The reading didn't go the way I thought it would. I thought we would talk more about motherhood and my stress. We did, but in a completely different way than I ever imagined. Sonia said I was meant to attend Translucent You in 2008. In fact, she said, my going was by Divine Appointment. She went on to explain that Divine Appointments are preplanned meetings set up by God before we are born and they are connected to what we are meant to do in life, to our purpose. It was no mistake that I had been drawn to that particular conference for years. I was supposed to go. Attending Translucent You felt right to me, but I was hesitant about figuring out the logistics of being able to go. I actually mentioned this to Sonia directly towards the end of the reading. She repeated that my going was by Divine Appointment, so if I asked, the money and logistics would be taken care of—but I had to ask.

During our reading, Sonia picked up on my feelings of unworthiness and my own hesitation to trust myself. Attending Translucent You intuitively felt right for me, but I felt guilty about getting money from nothing. I wasn't permitted to work in Japan, and I didn't want to take money out of our family budget to go on this trip. Additionally, Translucent You still took place in Hawaii, so I would either have to take our daughter with me or get a full time sitter to watch her in Tokyo while I was gone (more expenses to cover). This reading was something of a test for me; it would be the first time I would have to believe in something that I couldn't see. I had to trust Sonia and I had to trust God/the Universe that if I took one step towards planning the trip, the Universe would bring the rest to me. What was really going on? This was my soul trying to communicate to me that the prayer I put out to God a few years earlier was in motion to be answered. Although I could not see it at the time, God was actually in the process of sending Janelle to me to teach me how to connect to the Divine. Sonia was the vehicle to bring her into my life. Remember, I was holding Sonia's book in my hand when I asked for help. God was trying to show me he was listening to every detail of my prayer.

The deadline for registration was in January and the class of thirty was filling up fast. So I decided to ask my husband if I could attend the conference.

It did not go well.

My usually very supportive husband laughed in my face and said, "Let me get this straight: you want me to take off work so you can go to Hawaii on vacation and I have to stay home and watch Sophia for a week either here or in Hawaii?" And I said, "It's a retreat, not a vacation, but yes." And he said no. So I gave him more information about the trip. The answer was still no.

More time passed. I still wondered how this Divine Appointment was going to happen. During this time, Dee had been working until three and four in the morning six or seven days a week. He had been working longer hours in Japan than he had ever worked in his career. That, combined with a new baby, was a lot for anyone to handle. I knew that between the two of us, he was probably the one in greater need of going to a retreat or on vacation. We also never really went on vacation when we lived in Asia. Most of our time off was spent once a year at home seeing family. His long hours at work and inability to take time off weighed heavily on my mind. I did feel guilty asking for this trip. I understood why he was saying no, but I also couldn't get the Divine Appointment comment that Sonia made out of my mind. Based on Dee's firm answer to my request, my going wasn't looking good. I decided to let the whole conversation go and started preparing for Christmas.

That year, we traveled back to the United States for the holidays so Sophia could spend time with her grandparents and with aunts and uncles on both sides of the family. We celebrated Christmas Day with my in-laws. I really wasn't wanting any presents because celebrating Christmas with my family was a gift in and of itself. However, my in-laws surprised me with a check on Christmas day. It happened to be for the exact amount of money I needed to cover the cost of the retreat in Hawaii, and to take Dee and Sophia if we chose to make it a family trip. As I opened the envelope and showed the check to my husband, the amount caught us both by surprise. My in-laws didn't know about our discussions surrounding Translucent You; in fact, no one knew about this trip but me and Dee. As we both looked at the check, I said to my husband, "Looks like Hawaii is now in our budget," and he agreed. The only thing left for me to do was to find a babysitter for Sophia. Once I shared my plans to go to Hawaii, my mom said she would meet us there and take care of Sophia. So in the span of twenty days from my reading with Sonia, the budget and babysitting were taken care of. I was really starting to believe wholeheartedly in the importance of this Divine Appointment.

When we returned to Japan in January, I registered for Translucent You just before it sold out. I learned I was pregnant with our second child during February of 2008, and I was thrilled for our family.

Translucent You 2008 (TY)

I met Janelle in the art room on the second day of Translucent You. Everyone attending TY was asked to create an art project during the week and present our work to the group at the closing ceremony. We were told we could create anything we wanted, but our piece had to be created from our soul and had to represent who we thought we were on a soul level at that time. Examples included poetry, short stories, photography, painting or even a dance. I was thrilled to finally be in Hawaii, but I was feeling extremely nervous that morning because I couldn't decide what to create for my final project. I saw Janelle in the art room, but we didn't know each other. We hadn't even introduced ourselves; I just saw her across the room.

I asked her what she was doing and she said she was painting a portrait of her soul. She kept on walking back and forth across the room between her canvas and the jars of paint colors in the middle of the room. She was mixing colors trying to get the exact shade of her soul. I kept on staring at her as she walked back and forth across the room. Staring at people wasn't something I typically did, especially after living in New York City and Tokyo where it was considered rude behavior, but there I was sitting at a table trying to figure out what my project would be and watching this tiny blonde woman paint, who was so happy and very sure of herself.

At one point she looked back at me, and I said that she reminded me of someone I knew in Tokyo. I thought they looked a bit like one another. She actually said no, that it was not the familiarity of the way she looked, but her energy that I was drawn to. Honestly, the comment went over my head. I was still stressed out over my project, and I couldn't get my mind to settle down. I knew I wanted to paint something but couldn't figure out what to paint or even how to get started. I was letting this small project that was only part of the week-long conference stress me out instead of empowering me. Even worse, my stress was preventing me from enjoying the moment, the people in front of me, and the conference.

Janelle noticed my uneasiness and casually started asking me questions from across the room about what I wanted to paint. When I started to share some of my ideas she came over to my small table, sat down and asked me more questions about how I felt when I painted pictures. I started to tell her that the last time I felt that I created anything from my soul was in kindergarten. Even though my twin brother and I were in the same class together, our teacher used to separate us so we could learn to play independently. When I had the opportunity to choose an activity on my own I always wanted to finger paint because it made me feel free and happy. I hoped that painting something at Translucent You would bring that feeling back. I ended up making a huge painting of different colored handprints because Janelle got me to see that when I paint I connect to my soul through my hands and that the connection comes through as a feeling. I didn't realize it at the time, but that was a healing session between us. Janelle was able to help me get out of my head, move through my fear and uneasiness, and get in touch with my heart so I could create from my higher self in that art room.

What happened in the art room was a microcosm of what Janelle and I would go on to do on *Spiritual Happy Hour*. I was letting a very small piece of the conference stop me from enjoying life, and I didn't know how to get around it. I was also very concerned with following the schedule and rules of the conference. I didn't talk to Janelle for the rest of the week because we were put into smaller groups of six, and she and I were placed in separate sections. Then during the last day of the conference, after our presentations, she sat down with me and I talked to her about Dee and Sophia and a bit about my pregnancy. I learned more about her family and her work. She gave me her card, and we stayed in touch over the next several months by telephone.

Jen and Janelle TY 2008

I felt more centered and balanced after the retreat and excited to return to Japan with Dee and Sophia. The next six months flew by as our son Matthew was born in November and we decided to move back to the United States in early 2009.

My friendship with Janelle really developed when I moved back to the States. She and I called each other all the time and I loved the fact that I could talk to her about raising children (nap time, introducing solid food to a baby, sibling rivalry), but I could also ask her questions about spirituality. I used to call her during the day when a bigger spiritual question would come to mind and we would talk about reincarnation, soul agreements, and the law of attraction. Janelle always answered my questions and would spend as much time on the phone as I needed. Even though she had ten thousand things going on in her own life, she made the time to talk. I used to joke with her that she was my own personal "bat phone." Our calls continued for about eight months and then came that fateful day in March when Janelle called to suggest that we co-host a radio show together.

The phone call—March, 2010

I remember the day clearly in my mind: it was March in New Jersey and it was cold and dreary outside. It was mid-morning, and I was home taking care of Sophia and Matthew. The phone rang. It was Janelle. The conversation was quick. Janelle said "Hey, we need to do a radio show together—me and you. You ask me questions everyone else wants to know, but no one will ask." She went on to say something like, "Our brains are completely opposite. I don't think the way you think. I'm so connected (to the Universe) that I don't have the kind of thoughts you have and my Team (meaning her guides) is telling me we need to do a radio show together. You ask me all the questions you want answers to and I will channel in the information... sound fun?"

Yes, it did sound fun and the thought of doing a radio show together resonated deeply within me on a soul level, but I also remember feeling afraid to do the show because initially I was afraid to speak publicly about my spiritual beliefs. Also, I had absolutely no idea how to get on the radio. All I knew was that I wanted to come together with Janelle and create this radio show, but I didn't realize I would learn so many life lessons in the process.

When I look back at our first three shows, I see now there was a tug of war going on inside me between my head and my heart. My heart was telling me this was a dream come true. Learning about the other side and how to incorporate intuition into my everyday life was my passion and having the opportunity to interview Janelle and get Divine guidance on a regular basis felt amazing. I had so many questions rolling around in my head about soul history, intuition, connection, and how to get Divine assistance for everyday life that I couldn't wait to begin. I researched on line radio stations, found a provider, and got an account about a week after our phone conversation. Then my head took over and fear started to creep in.

I started to question my ability to participate in the show and my worries soon turned into fear. I had a fear of standing in my own power, a fear of being seen in the world as my authentic self and of being worthy to stand next to and co-create with Janelle. Instead of turning inward and facing these fears head on, or calling Janelle to talk about them and make a plan together, I started to make excuses to myself as to why I couldn't start planning for the first show. I never backed out of doing the show—it really was something I wanted to do—but I just couldn't get myself to take the first step to start the conversation to plan the first show or get on the air. My excuses about my own abilities and worthiness included, "I don't know enough; I'm not intuitive enough; I'm not a good interviewer;" and, "I'm not qualified to manage the technical aspects of the show."

I also made excuses about how others would react: "People will think I'm crazy, and other moms won't talk to me at school pick-up," and "Is this really something a suburban mom does in her free time?" I was also afraid of how my extended family would react to the topics we explored on the show. How would they feel about my sharing about soul history and past lives in a public forum? Once the show was on the air what was broadcast could not be taken back. I wondered if my spiritual views would affect their lives in a negative way.

Deep down, I knew *Spiritual Happy Hour* was going to be successful and that scared me. I knew Janelle was completely different from any other intuitive I had met or worked with. Janelle lives life "full out." She doesn't shy away from new adventures even if they scare her, and she also doesn't diminish her light while serving other people. She is her authentic self, and she's not afraid of how she shows up. Co-creating with such a powerful, loving person was scary for me. I knew in saying yes to doing the show that I would have to step into this role for myself both on and off the show. I would also have to own my own power and trust my own intuition and my own connection. Once I knew all the answers to my questions, I would have to really start taking responsibility for my life from a soul level, which would be different from what I had been doing up until that point. I would have to stop playing victim, stop living small and start really co-creating what I wanted. I would not be able to go back to the way I was living before the show. To do all of this, I would also have to be more vulnerable than I'd ever been in all areas. I would have to take a chance on the unknown and put my trust in what I couldn't see but what felt right in my heart.

Doing this privately in my relationships was scary enough, but doing it on the radio took my spiritual development to a whole other level.

Janelle's thoughts on doing the show together

The amazing part of calling Jen about the show was that I was as nervous about proposing the idea as she was about considering it. A surge of thoughts went through my mind, from "What if she doesn't get it?" to "What if she says no?" I actually was afraid. This was very new to me, to ask that someone be part of a very intimate part of my life. It meant I had to trust while asking for support. I knew Jen had no idea the amount of tears and pure peace she gave back to me. It was my first test in realizing I could not make this journey alone. Part of my education—meaning what I needed to get—was again blind faith; not faith in God, but faith in a person. Could I be patient with myself? Could I let go and allow someone to really see me, warts and all?

During the taping of the shows, I had to get really comfortable with my style of channeling information. All of my "ticks," like saying "Uh" or "You know" right before a channeled moment. Were people going to understand what was happening? It is not very easy to follow at first. This was my perfectionism coming up for me to work on. Oh and the final tick: I don't get notes on how the conversation is going to go down. Dang it, I wanted notes or at least a heads up. Not a chance. Again, I had to go in blind to each show, trusting that I would have the information that I needed at the right time. *Well that was fantastic.* I did finally let go and allow.

Letting Jennifer into my internal process scared me because it was such a private relationship between my guides, God, and my soul. So as usual, I jumped in, feeling all the unsavory raw emotions and not controlling any of it. I let Jen take the reins; for the first time, I let a person lead me. I wanted to be present to her, to witness her spiritual unfolding. That is my love. In turn I gained a trusted friend. That's big for me. I felt supported fully in the physical world.

As we journeyed from show to show, different lessons would come up for me around the show's theme, mainly because I had to walk the walk to understand fully the message. What Jen never knew was each time I let her push me into a deep understanding of my gifts. She led me to fully grasp messages about life here while holding me in a supportive light. That support allowed me to fully anchor all my spiritual knowledge here. The process gave me a safety net to dive deeper so I could bring more to people. I know that it had been God's plan all along to pair me with Jen to create a bridge between both worlds. And truly, it was as easy and enjoyable as having conversation with a girlfriend about clothes.

Funny moments by Jen

We broadcast the first couple of shows from my kitchen, and found out in the middle of the shows that it wasn't the best environment for us because it was far from quiet. Dee and I live about a mile away from a small commuter airport and even though the windows were closed the day we were broadcasting, you could hear planes flying overhead. It was a very high traffic day for a December. I ended up moving upstairs to our son Matthew's room because it seemed to be the quietest room in the house. So Keith, our sound guy, and I seated ourselves on small chairs at a kids' table and began taping. So, here we were talking about deep spiritual topics in front of the awe-inspiring audience of my son's stuffed animals, which totally fit with Janelle's saying that Life is a Playground.

Funny moments by Janelle

Okay, so by this time we knew there would be lessons to learn on both our sides. There were moments when Jen wanted to throw in the towel. We had mic issues, computer malfunctions, and phone issues. I would call in and Jen would be angry because she couldn't hear. The big joke is that's what she is always trying to do—hear her Team. There was static on the show like, "Umm are you hearing us?"

Then came the day I called in several times from the very same number I always call in on. No answer. I thought, "What the heck?" I checked the number for blog radio a couple more times. Surely she sees it's my number, I thought. I decided to text her on her phone. She finally got the message. How in the heck did she not know my number, the Bat phone? We laughed because this became the marker of our journey—not seeing what was right in front of us.

More funny moments by Jen

To say we had mic issues is Janelle being really kind. I would completely freak out before some of our shows, literally jumping up and down and telling God that if he wanted this show to happen, he'd have to send help. Meanwhile, on Janelle's side she could SEE all the Divine Helpers around me trying to get the messages through, but I was so uptight and not breathing that I couldn't see, hear, or feel what I needed to do next. Usually, my husband would pop upstairs and figure it out—so between Janelle asking for more divine help and Dee working the cables, we would get on air. I am grateful to both of them for sticking with me.

There was part of me that was so happy that we were on radio and not video because as Janelle would channel in really profound information, I would make so many "huh" faces. I was sincerely trying to understand and grasp what was being said AND come up with a follow up question. I would literally have silent quick conversations with myself, "Did she just say THAT?" and then I'd realize she had continued on for another few sentences—all of which I missed because I was trying to catch up at the same time.

What was a wonderful gift for me that Janelle just let me learn and didn't criticize my reaction to her channeling. I could "get it" in my own time, even if that meant fumbling over a concept. Janelle always found a way to use my learning process to dive deeper into each topic. I am so grateful to have been given such a loving and safe environment to learn what holds us back in life.

In doing the show, I realized that it wasn't the ability to predict the future that I'd been looking for my whole life, but the ability to *connect to the Divine* that I wanted most. I had never lost my connection—none of us do—but my *fears* about life were getting in the way of my ability to use my intuition with consistency. I *wanted* to connect but couldn't get out of my own way of my own *thoughts and fears* in order to do so. I realize now connecting to the Divine really means connecting to the Divine in Heaven but *also with the Divine in myself.*

I had the pleasure of visiting Janelle at her home in Texas several times during the process of our putting this book together. On the last night of my last visit we sat across from each other in her office laughing and talking about our friendship, the show, and this book. Mid-laugh, Janelle tilted her head ever so slightly and said, "Hold on, hold on… listen to what they just revealed to me," ("they" being her Team of Spiritual Guides). She said, "They are telling me my relationship with them is equal to your relationship with your twin brother. The way you feel connected to your twin brother is equal to the way that I've felt connected to God and my Guides my whole life."

As Janelle started to give me more of an explanation, the feeling of the message her guides were conveying to us came into my body. In that moment, I could *feel* the depth and trust of her connection to them. I understood the strength of that connection; the trust, the emotion, the joy, and the laughter they share together, because I've felt that feeling many times before—not with God, but with my brother. I have one hundred percent unspoken trust and faith in my brother Jon. I never question his word. If he says he is going to do something for me, I trust it will be done. My belief in him is solid because it is based on shared history. I am also one hundred percent myself with my brother. I don't hold back who I am with him and this is what makes our connection so strong.

Around the age of five, my brother and I were not allowed to be together in the same classroom at school. We were expected to find our independence away from one another. Not wanting to lose the feeling of our special connection, I started to look to other children to recreate the bond we shared together. The inner nudging that I felt as a child began at the same time that I was encouraged to find my independence. I now know that nudging was actually my Soul trying to form a Divine partnership with me to guide me in my life, but I was too young at the time to understand what was going on.

Partnering with Janelle on *Spiritual Happy Hour* taught me how to reconnect in partnership with the Divine. The message that Janelle channeled that last night in her office served as a powerful reference point for me, because I could finally gauge the depth of the faith and trust Janelle places in her relationship with God and her Guides. It also provided a way for me to measure my lack of faith in my own relationship with God. Up until that time, I thought I was putting one hundred percent of my faith in God, but really I was probably only putting in twenty to thirty percent. I may have put out requests to God, but I know I never gave Him one hundred percent faith and trust that what I wanted for myself would occur in my life. Reconnecting with my Divine Partnership and understanding the depth of faith that I needed to have in the partnership was one of the missing links to feeling the special connection I'd been searching for my whole life.

The other piece I learned was that I had to do my part in this Divine Partnership. I had to take action on the messages I was given. Janelle has a back and forth conversation throughout her day with God and her Team of guides. She has faith in the guidance she receives and then she makes a choice to take action with the message she's received and that helps her accomplish her life's goals. I've learned that Divine Partnership is a choice. Janelle taught me that we always have a choice: we can put our faith in the guidance we receive and take action, or we can ignore it. It is always a choice. That's Divine Partnership.

INTRODUCTION
THIS IS WHAT
Spiritual Happy Hour IS

Spiritual Happy Hour is more than a radio show; it is sacred shared space—between Janelle, her Team, me, my guides from the other side—and you, the receiver of this information. For me, it is a celebration of the soul and a coming together for the benefit of all. I bring the human aspect to the show with my wanting to understand how to incorporate guidance from the other side, so I can solve problems and generally live a happier life. I bring a sincere need to know how things work.

Janelle is a living demonstration of how to live with one foot, so to speak, in both the spiritual and the material world. Janelle brings the Divine perspective; she brings the wisdom, the knowledge, and the understanding of our unlimited potential. She lives, works and breathes from the heart. She is one hundred percent authentic in who she is and in her love for life and for everyone in it. She knows no boundaries, she sees no limits, she is free flowing, loving and quick moving, yet super fun and powerful at the same time. Helping people is her passion. She can see all of our potential, all of our thoughts, our history, our dreams, our faults and misgiving, and she believes in us and in who we are, and in what we want to be. She doesn't judge us; instead, she holds space for us and sends us support to see hardships as opportunities to learn and grow so that we can bring our dreams—what we really want for ourselves—into our reality and create Heaven on Earth.

About how this book is written:

This book is divided into four sections. Each section contains the word-for-word transcripts from three radio shows that are linked together by a common topic. Bracketed around these transcripts, Janelle and I share about some of the issues that each of us were pondering during the time the shows were broadcast, and what we've come to understand looking back from the shows. Many of the lessons I learned are repeated, as they surfaced in different areas of my life to be addressed from the perspective of being a wife, sister, mother, friend, and so on.

In addition, following the printed transcript of each show, I share a brief breakdown of the corresponding numerological Life Path Numbers and the lessons associated with each them. I began studying numerology before we started broadcasting *Spiritual Happy Hour*. Numerology was founded by Pythagoreas and is based on his belief that numbers carry vibration and can be associated with positive and negative character traits.

To calculate the Life Path Number of each show, I added up the day, month and year each show was broadcast and reduced the sum down to a single digit number (or 11, 22, or 33) and applied what I learned about the character traits associated with that number to the lessons that were channeled in during each show.

When I looked at all the numbers as a whole I realized that there was a pattern in the first part of the series and it is as follows from show 1 to 7. The Life Path numbers for each show, in order are: 4, 11, 1, 6, 4, 11, 1. I found it fascinating that the energy behind shows 1, 2, and 3 was repeated in shows 5, 6 and 7. When you read the chapters, you will come up with your own interpretation of lessons and how they relate to the Life Path Numbers.

One final thing to keep in mind is that Janelle and I made the deliberate choice to keep the text of each transcript "as is"— meaning that what you read is for the most part exactly how it was spoken on the show. Janelle channeled in all her information live on the air and as a result, she pauses frequently as she is "downloading" information. Many times she will say the words "you know" or "um" to signify a pause in the conversation. At those times she was getting more information about the topic at hand. My reactions have also been kept "as is." You'll notice that I tend to use the words "wow" and "fantastic" a lot. This was my true reaction to the channeled information. I had never heard or thought about many of the concepts that Janelle shared during the shows and many times my brain needed some time to catch up with what was being said and in order to formulate a follow up question.

Spiritual Happy Hour originally aired on Friday afternoons at 1pm Eastern time and noon Central time. We chose the middle of the day because it was a quieter time around my house and because we wanted people to tune in while they were at work. We also wanted to give them the experience of Happy Hour coming earlier in the day and help them start their weekend in a fun way. Janelle and I usually spoke by phone at the beginning of each week to choose a topic for the upcoming show. Then, during the call, we would ask each other what was going on in each of our lives that week to see if something in particular was on our minds. We would both suggest topics to each other and then together we'd decide which one felt more inspired or intuitively right.

When we first started doing the show, I was confused about my role. I would ask questions about specific situations that I was struggling with in my own life, and I felt selfish because Janelle and her Team answered every single one of them. At the time, I was struggling with three or four central recurring themes that included abundance, intention, procrastination, partnership, and self-worth. Many times I would find myself asking Janelle the same questions over and over again week after week.

My conversations with Janelle gave the chance to see how the struggles that were playing out in different areas of my life were not separate, but energetically interconnected and therefore manifesting in all facets of my being. So, for example, I knew I wasn't being totally vulnerable in my marriage but I thought I was in friendships. What I was shown through the show was the opposite—how my unwillingness to be vulnerable affected *every* relationship I had in some way. I needed to pay attention and really *feel* what was going on; not just think about it.

I really wish I could say that I got every lesson immediately after we finished each show, but it didn't happen that way. It has been a three-part process for me that took three years to complete and I'm still incorporating those lessons into my life now. For me, I had to first hear the information directly from Janelle on the show, read the transcripts to incorporate the messages that were conveyed during each show, then write about it. This book is the net result of that integration, and it is our deepest hope that you take this gift of two polar opposite people walking through their own integration of spiritual lessons that enabled them to grow more connected to themselves and apply that in your own way and that you allow it to move you as it has us.

4

CHAPTER ONE
BLACK AND TAN
"FEAR"

Show 1 – Soul vs. Spirit
Show 2 – Ushering in the Golden Age
Show 3 – What Holds You Back from Starting Something New

The first three shows Janelle and I broadcast together were all about spiritual foundation. In show 1, "Soul vs. Spirit," Janelle talks about who we really are and what we are here to accomplish at this time on Earth. Show 2 addressed the idea of "Ushering in the Golden Age," and understanding the steps we need to take to get there. Show 3 was titled, "What Holds You Back from Starting Something New." The messages channeled in these shows inspired me to turn my attention to my own foundation in my life partnerships and to look at where I formed my first partnerships.

While I truly love partnership, I've come to realize that I have a pattern of giving my authority away and taking on the role of helper in many of the relationships I form. Being partnered with and sharing such a special connection with my twin brother Jon was an integral part of my life. It is hard for me to explain what it feels like to have someone by your side facing every new experience with you and supporting your every struggle since the time you were born. It felt at times like we lived in our own world, aware that life was going on around us, but so focused on what we were doing together that we didn't notice. I never felt alone. Throughout our childhood, Jon was facing the same milestones that I was and it gave me comfort and reassurance that I could learn and master new things, because I witnessed him doing the same. When he mastered something, I felt happy for him and *inspired* to try the same thing for myself. We were never competitive with one another, but considered ourselves equals and gave each other complete support.

Things changed for me when we went to preschool because I had no interest in going and wanted to stay home with our mom, but Jon couldn't wait to go. From that time on, he became our leader and would figure out the way the world worked for the two of us, like a second mother. I started to let him make decisions for me, despite how much our own mother tried to get me to think for myself. As I moved through childhood and into young adulthood, I transferred this pattern into the friendships I formed. I started to use some of my friendships for guidance and security more than as a space to share, learn and grow. Because I associated strong leadership with my brother, I gravitated toward both kids and adults who were stronger leaders in personality than I was at the time. I went along (for the most part) with everyone else's ideas, never really contributing my thoughts first. I always found out what the other person's opinion was and then based my opinion on what they said. I thought agreeing with what others wanted would bring that same feeling of connectedness to the friendship, but that never worked.

The first three *Spiritual Happy Hour* shows taught me that support in partnership doesn't come from allowing the other person to tell you what to do; it comes from your own ability to be vulnerable, open, and honest with yourself first so you will have the courage to openly share your authentic self with others. This is a time in history where we are meant to get in touch with who we are meant *to be* in this lifetime; not what we are meant to do, but who our soul really is. We all have gifts and talents encoded into our DNA that are uniquely ours and we need to share those parts of ourselves with the world. When we share authentically in that way, our spirit connects to our body and raises our vibration and the vibration of those around us.

The partnerships we make from this space stand apart from all others and inspire us to create our soul's work. I shared in this way with my twin brother but didn't do this in my other relationships growing up. I didn't realize that the "key ingredient" to that special connection was being independent, sharing who you really are, and not holding back your true self. I never before shared from that space; instead, I had spent all my energy focused on other people and got tired and frustrated because I was not allowing my own gifts and talents to be witnessed, validated, and shared. My spirit wasn't fully present either and I never got to create from that space. Sharing my authentic self would have allowed me to remain independent while still being partnered. And that, alone, may have brought on the connection I had been looking for most of my life.

Janelle's perspective on the first three shows

So here is what I find interesting: most people have a preconceived idea about becoming spiritual. They believe that you somehow don't have fears if you're spiritual. But it's not that you don't face fears; it's that consciousness involves you to look at fear in a different way. Many times in my journey, fear has landed in my lap. Sometimes it's easier for me to look at it than

7

others. The emotion of fear can cause us to feel unsafe, leaving us wanting to control things. Let me give you an example: When I spoke to a large group for the first time, I was definitely feeling fear. I used that fear to help me grow deeply connected to my authentic self. Fear is not there to stop you as much as it used to be in times of survival. Now it is a commonly misunderstood emotion. When used properly, fear can help us delve deeply into our subconscious thoughts. So I want to make it clear, I'm not a thrill seeker. I like what happens when I discover what's on the other side of that fear that seemed so big. Honestly, it's that I don't like to be defined or put in a box. Next time you have a fear, try to push through to see what lies on the other side.

Show 1 – Soul vs. Spirit
Air Date: December 14, 2012
Life Path number 4

Jen: *Janelle, can you tell us what you do because your work is so different from what other intuitives and healers are doing.*

Janelle: Sure, Jen. I'm so excited that we're on this journey together and you know, laying some groundwork for others, you know, and for information to come out there that's not out there yet. For me, you know, the experience of working with people and working with groups is more of a multidimensional experience. So, I'm not just talking to the mind or to the emotions, but I also feel the body and also, you know, connect with you individually in a unique way and for me, it's my life's passion; my passion is people and life and to help them live a different way.

Jen: *Can you talk about how you were born connected and how you never lost that connection to The Divine?*

Janelle: Absolutely. I think in my experience. I was taught by The Universe. When I was 2 and 3 years old, I was having past lifetime experiences. I was having conversations with my angels and guides. I was, you know, receiving psychic information. I did not know that this was anything different from anyone else's experience. It wasn't until I hit teenage years that I realized, "Hey, you know what, not everyone hears that conversation," or "not everyone feels that way" or "not everyone knows in that knowing way," and what I find with most people is either you grow with your spiritual gifts or at around 12 or 13, you choose to let go of them and come back to them as an adult. It's never the case that you just disconnect altogether and don't ever go back because the soul has a longing to always come back to that original connection; what you were born with. That's why if you look at babies, they have bright beautiful love coming from them, but that was, I think, why I was meant to teach and work with people is because that connection for me was never inhibited, you know. You can say if you look at me I'm a little bit child-like in a lot of ways and that's the way it is. It's very free, it's very non-judgmental, you know, and part of what I think what we're meant to do is go back to that.

Jen: *We are all born with so many gifts and so much to share with others, but we forget them along the way. Can you break it down for us? What is Spirit? What does Spirit mean to you? What does that mean to us? How can we remember what we were meant to do?*

Janelle: Well, I would say, you know, for me, it's like when I look at someone's eyes and they either look checked out or they're home. And the home presence, it looks like a fire, a light, like a brilliance in their eyes and the physical feeling is they are joyful; they are peaceful within themselves. And so for me, when I look at someone, that's what I see in them. First I look at their eyes and then I feel their body to see if their spirit is home, and that's why I said the feeling is a peaceful nurturing place. And then the other thing, too, is I think for most people, not knowing and really I think most of us don't know when our spirit is home or what they even feel like.

Jen: *I think it's hard to understand how that feels differently. If we are born "all in" in Spirit as babies, when do we start to lose that connection and how do we figure out what we need to do to* *bring ourselves back in, to get that feeling, to understand what that is?*

Janelle: You know, it's so true, I mean, because, you know, that's why I say when you look at babies, they're just so brilliant and so full of life, you know. And I say, you know, one, it's a combination of things. It's life, you know, that kind of pushes you down and then also, too, on a biological level when babies come in, there is a conduit that connects them to the universe all the time. And so, as that kind of soft spot in their brain closes, they start kind of going into the space of losing that a little bit. And through family situations or through what I call life, whatever the case may be, the child will move into adulthood and become less and less familiar with the spirit in the sense of how that feels because emotions come in, hormones come in, you know, family situations, expectations, and all of that. We're less free as we become adults, we're less free to just be. And so, how you know in your body, it feels like, almost like, a melancholy kind of feeling like you're just doing your day, you know what I'm saying? Like it's just...

Jen: *...a dull feeling. You might feel dull.*

Janelle: Yes. Like you're just doing your day. And also, too, you can look at your own eyes and see if you have that fire, you have that—it's unmistakable when you see it—and when you feel your spirit back home in your body. It will always, your spirit will always lead you back to that place. So, I call it reference point, you know, once you have that reference point within your body again, you will know absolutely when you're not.

Jen: *A few months ago we had a conversation about spirit being in and out of your body, and I asked you, "Once a person's spirit leaves, how do you get it back in or where did it go?" You said "It's not where did it go; it's more what do I need to do to get it back in?" It must be like sleepwalking to not be all in.*

Janelle: Yes, it's very much true. And that's what I say, you know. It's not necessarily like you can become completely always aware that your spirit is disconnected. It's more of what do you need to do to enhance that connection today in your body. The thing is, we replenish ourselves at night, right? So, the spirit kind of goes and gets replenished and that's why you hear people say sometimes that they have that, when they wake up, they feel disoriented. It is because the spirit isn't fully into the body yet when you first wake up. And everyone does that at night; everyone's spirit leaves and goes and gets replenished and comes back in. But to what degree are you allowing your spirit to come in, is more of what the occurrence is, right. So, you can be 5% in or 2% in or 75% in; it's all up to you and the choices that you make through the day. How emotional you are, or whatever stressful circumstances you're working through, or if you have that physical illness that can also make your spirit kind of leave and check out.

Jen: *Okay. Or, vice-versa, if you are loving and you are surrounding yourself with experiences and people you love, is that the time where your spirit jumps back in?*

Janelle: So true. Laughter is something that brings your spirit back in, you know, how like you when you laugh, and then you laugh with such a belly laugh that you just feel all over joy, that's your spirit being fully present.

Jen: *Janelle, when you work with young kids (ages 6, 7, 8, 9) can you see when they start to lose their connection? Or to what degree the connection is becoming limited?*

Janelle: Absolutely. You know, like I said, you know, especially with kids, it's almost more clear than it is with adults. I mean, it kind of makes sense, you know, because as adults, we have more stuff, but with kids, they are clear in general and so it's easier to see with them, and what I find with kids is if they're in a stressful home situation or if they're limiting themselves, because you know, kids are their own being, you know, they have their own journey here and they may be limiting themselves or afraid to express themselves freely and that doesn't come from their family situations. Yes, you can see it absolutely with kids; you can see it. Not so much in babies, you know, really up until two years old, they're solidly connected. And then, some of the new kids that are being born today, I don't see it as much as when I first started working, you know, with kids and parents and seeing all of that shifting. But it is really clear.

Jen: *If you're in a family or work situation and you're someone who is all in (or fully connected) but you are surrounded by coworkers who are not connected, how do you maintain your state of connection? Can they bring you down? Does it depend on each situation?*

Janelle: Well, you know, I think it's so important that you brought up the work situation because I think it's one of—you know, we spend most of our time at work, you know. It's the other marriage that we have and I think with people at work in a work situation, it can go either/or. Sometimes they can take away from you if there's something you're needing to learn about being connected with people and relationships and stuff like that, and so, they can enhance you and you enhance them and raise them up. The goal is to have a two-party system where you raise them up and they raise you up; that no one leaves feeling inadequate in any way, and so, through conversation or through doing tasks together, we learn about the nature of relationship and how it connects to our spirit, and the spirit only wants to just serve the best interest of everyone, including yourself. So, when you get into different situations, it will try to encourage you to listen to what really needs to happen and serve your spirit in all situations, and it may not be the most comfortable thing, but a normal thing.

Jen: *When we're trying to listen to our spirit how do we know that the guidance we are receiving is really our spirit and not "just coincidence"?*

Janelle: I say, for me, there are two things that happen. First off, if there's something that is compromising your spirit, a situation, an emotion or a thought that you're having, it will—most of the time, when I see it, it hits you in the gut, you have a gut reaction, "Oh okay, this doesn't feel right." So, the next stage of that is okay, spirit works in very subtle, subtle conversations. It's never going to intrude in your life; it's never going to harm you and you know, it has your best interest at mind always and it is very subtle. It can occur like your own thought. The way that you know is, your spirit will communicate with you in a very utmost, I want to say, non-emotional way. So, that's why I say, sometimes it occurs like your own thought until you get comfortable with the feeling. It will "ping." I say it pings through your body. You'll feel it in your body like a bell; some people feel it as waves of truth, you know, like that kind of thing when all the hair stands up on your body;

that's the other one. Those moments are your spirit communicating with you to let you know, "Hey, you know, this is a good situation" or "This is what you need to do next" and so for hearing-wise, it may come through conversation with other people that you have an "aha" moment.

Jen: *For example, you're in a coffee shop and happen to overhear somebody giving advice about a question that you were thinking about? There it is.*

Janelle: Yes, yes, yes. Sometimes, it can come from outside influences in that sense, you know, it's a direct message for you. Because we're not always present enough, like I said, to hear it; to know, and until you become comfortable and your spirit becomes comfortable communicating with you, it might use other people to bring those messages to you. Absolutely.

Jen: *Another question just popped into my head. What do your guides say about technology and being connected or disconnected? Is technology helping or harming? Is it harming our connection when we're tuned in to our iPhones and iPads? Is it harder for them these days to get through to us?*

Janelle: Well, I think, it's, you know, it's a two-part question because in one sense, they can bring you the information and you know, they can use the internet to do so. The second part of that is, that it may not be—you may have addictive behavior so you may be on it too much and block your signal, that's the other thing. Because the internet and all of that stuff, media, and all of that, is frequencies and that's how the universe and our spirit connects with us is through frequency. It's tuning in to a different frequency in order to connect that way, so yeah, its two-part. One

15

is they can use it to bring you things that you need and I have seen that happen even with my own self, but the other part of it is if you're so connected and wired in, you become ungrounded in a way and it is harder for a spirit to get that information to us sometimes. So, it can go both ways. To serve and it can prevent.

Jen: *Okay. And then in the same way, Janelle, I'm wondering when we go through great stressors in our lives like natural disasters, a job switch or a job loss or a death in the family or an illness, I would think that these would be times when our connection to Spirit should be very strong, but that's not always the case. What do you think about that? How do we stay connected in times of stress?*

Janelle: Well, that's a, you know, that's a unique perspective in the sense of, you know, when I have stressors in my own life, I look at them as "Okay, well this is obviously something that I need to learn and grow from" so my spirit stays always connected to it. But for most people, when they experience stressors and outside influences that cause them to be in a place that they didn't think they would be in, or either they'll, you know, go through disaster; those kinds of stresses will cause your spirit to leave if you're not paying attention to what those situations actually mean. Like there is a lesson in it; sometimes it's meaning you need to slow down, sometimes it means that you need to go out and give to other people, that you were so focused on yourself. All of these situations are meant to help us stay connected to the spirit and your spirit within. And so, the best way that I can suggest that you remain connected to your spirit during those times is, one, through prayer, and asking for assistance to not go into negative thought patterns or negative emotions in and around that situation, and to know that even though you're in that situation that you are still connected to a whole group of people so you have support. And I also, at this point in my life, just because I've been through so many different stressful situations, know that they know exactly what's going on in our life in the sense of the angels and the universe. In that sense and also, your soul has some consciousness as to "okay, well this was going to happen anyway," so, it's not that your life is being unseen or unwitnessed.

I think that they use our life to help bring us more connection to our authentic self, which is spirit in the body.

Jen: *It seems like there are so many people struggling right now. It feels as though people go through multiple stressors in a span of months to years. For example, a death in the family followed by a job loss, and then a natural disaster. Could you speak a little bit about that? Is that a trend that you see?*

Janelle: Yes, but I see it more now. I see more like whereas before when I first started working, you know, I may see one life-changing circumstance show up in a person's life. Now, I see four and five major life events at one time in a person's life. And I know without a doubt those, you know, series of events or stages of events in one period of, you know, like four to six months or even sometimes within a month, that those aren't meant for us to have our freak out moments, you know, even though we are going to because we're, you know, we're emotional beings, right? So, we have to have our freak outs and get right back into the game and really stay connected to that energy that we are. I think it's to help us remember what is really important to us, which is love and connecting with other people and serving the greater good, and also loving yourself.

Jen: *That's a huge point, a huge point.*

Janelle: I think that's the major point in those circumstances. If you have four or five situations, or even one, that it's meant to teach you, maybe to slow down and maybe to love yourself a little bit more and maybe be a little more patient with yourself and your experience of the world, and less about the outside and searching for the answers outside but searching for them within because you are your own guide.

Jen: *The experience is stripping you down again to where you were as a baby or a child. So you ask the questions why am I here, what am I supposed to do, where does this leave me now?*

Janelle: Yes, absolutely, absolutely. Because again, remember, it is about the life experiences that we have that kind of push us away from, "Oh, who was I when I was younger? What did I like to do? What made me happy?" and really, there was nothing outside of you that made you happy, you were just happy. I mean, if you look at kids, they are just happy. They're like "La-la-la" just playing around, you know, they don't care what other people think, you know, they're just happy in their body.

Jen: *Right, right. Exactly. Yeah, absolutely. Janelle, do you mind if we go ahead, I want to take a pause and we have a lot of callers that I think would love to talk with you about this topic or about a question or two. Is that okay with you?*

Janelle: Yeah, sounds really great. I'm so excited!

Jen: *Okay, alright. So, I'm going to put the first caller on now for your first reading, then anybody waiting to speak with Janelle. After that caller we will take a music break and then we'll hop* *right back in and we'll start taking calls from the call cue in the chatroom.*

Janelle: Okay. All right, let me just step in with you real quick. All right, so the first thing that jumps up at me is that you're working on, what they're saying to me is, becoming more self-confident in who you are and being more out into the world. And then, they're also telling me, too, that there's a little bit of, for you, understanding and being in relationships so a little bit of that specific comes up.

Caller #1: Okay.

Janelle: And there is a portion for you with this, like coming out and being more available for people, like in friendships and stuff like that in the world that has a little bit of a tie to money, because it feels like I want to expand what you do. And I feel like you're holding yourself back in a sense in that way and I almost want to tell you, you know exactly what I'm talking about because this idea has been rolling around in your thoughts for quite a while. I would say almost like three years, so it's definitely time to step up and get busy with that.

Caller #1: Okay. I am a technical consultant and I do partner with stores when people need help with their Mac's, their iPhones and things like that, but the one thing I have been focusing on for a while is the way to expand the reach of people, so people would know that there is someone like me available as a resource to them, and I have had some challenges, you know, putting that out there. So I've been looking for marketing that makes things like that, but that's probably what you're reading.

19

Janelle: Yeah, yeah. So, let me help you with that just real quick if you don't mind.

Caller #1: Sure.

Janelle: First. Because I have a whole unique distinction when it comes to understanding marketing, okay? And it is about, if you know clearly what your target person is, the person that you need to help, if you're clear about that, who your client is...

Caller #1: I am.

Janelle: Second, are you clear and in line with what it is that you want to help people with? Do you believe in it?

Caller #1: Yes, wholeheartedly. I would still do this if I won the lottery.

Janelle: See? Yeah, that's the same thing for me, right? Yeah, yeah, yeah, it's the same thing for me, this is my passion, right? So, the thing is when you have those two things in line, what I want you to get comfortable with is this, speaking outside and this is why they brought that up, speaking outside of your current networking group, not friends and all of that. What I'm saying is they want to put in your circumstances where like let's say you go to dinner and someone starts talking to you about computers whatever and you give them a card. That's the best form of marketing there is.

Caller #1: Okay.

Janelle: When they can build a personal relationship with you in a sense of, "Oh yeah, I met this guy at dinner and this is what he does."

Caller #1: Okay.

Janelle: That's what I want you to start doing.

Caller #1: Okay, I'll work more on that.

Janelle: That is your next stage and that's what I'm seeing about the abundance part of it coming in because it's not about the money for you in a sense, but I want you to be more well taken care of than you are right now.

Caller #1: Okay. I would like that for me as well.

Janelle: So, it's that in a sense, you know, and think about it like this. This is the Universe's way of kind of making sure that you have more freedom than you have now.

Caller #1: And that is one of the things I would like to be able to afford myself and for my family.

Janelle: Yeah, yeah, yeah. A little bit of travel, a little more fun, yeah.

Caller #1: Actually, what we're working on right now is a little more, a few more children, so I'm hoping with the eggs that we have on ice right now. we're going to have success early next year.

Janelle: I think so. Do you have kids right now?

Caller #1: I have one daughter, yes.

Janelle: Okay. I'm actually seeing there is potential for three kids but I'm not sure if it's including the one that you already have that's why I asked you about kids.

Caller #1 I would say so. We actually have two fertilized embryos that the doctor "is in love with" and we're looking to get started you know early next year.

Janelle: February. February.

Caller #1: Get started in February?

Janelle: I would say start looking at it in February, yeah.

Caller #1: Okay. Okay.

Janelle: Just start looking at it, playing around with the idea in February.

Jen: *Wow maybe twins?*

Caller #1: Well, that's what we were talking about but yeah, then we actually were talking about either next month or February so that's funny.

Janelle: Yeah, yeah, yeah. And it could possibly be twins and then you have another one after that.

Caller #1: That would be four then.

Janelle: Yeah, that's why I said I didn't know if it was three including the one you have or three in addition to.

Caller#1: Okay. I'll be happy if there's just three and done, you know, that'll be a good number.

Janelle: But you know, your test in this life is really how to maintain balance and not get so stressed. So, I wouldn't be surprised if they throw you a curveball and send you an extra one just for fun.

Caller#1: That would be great.

Janelle: All right. Thank you for letting me jump in there and go on a new journey, you know. I appreciate it.

Caller#1: Well, thank you, Janelle. It was good to speak with you today.

Janelle: Yeah, yeah, yeah. Great stuff. Thank you.

Jen: *All right, great. What we'll do is, we're just going to play a short song from Mark Stanton Welch called "Your Heart's Desire" and as were doing that, right as he finished, we're going to jump right back in to the calls.*

Janelle: All right.

Jen: *Okay, we're back and we have a question from a caller from New Jersey, okay, go ahead.*

Caller #2: Hi. Hi Janelle. I have a question regarding chemical and biological imbalances in your chemistry makeup and how that affects the spirit's ability to come in or just, you know, affect our lives.

Janelle: That's a great question because that's something that, you know, I haven't really talked to many people about, you know, in my field, about that particularly because it shows up in a very unique way for me. For me, what I see when I connect with someone who has that issue is that the neurons, like I can actually see the firing in the brain, not working the same way and what I often run into is sometimes that diagnostics is there, but it's really because the spirit is disconnected that causes that to show up. And so the more that you get back connected to your original, you know, connection to who you are, the more that you will see those sometimes decrease.

Caller #2: Do I need to get in touch with more of my spiritual side and then...?

Janelle: Yes.

Caller#2: Right. Well, I'm obviously asking about myself so...

Janelle: Yeah, yeah, yeah. No, totally, I get that. No, what I'm saying is that exactly what's happening is, it's called, there's a word for it that they're giving me but I can't get through it now, but disconnecting from your spiritual self and from your spirit actually causes you to have a chemical imbalance both hormonally and neurologically. And so, you don't react to situations in the same way because of that issue. So, the more that you engage with growing spiritually and getting back connected to who you were originally, you know, probably, 15, you know, 15 or so years ago. Then, because that's what I would say, would be a pivotal point for you when your energy shifted.

Caller #2: Oh I see.

Janelle: And you'll know exactly what that place is and that's when the symptoms started showing up, is then. It's not that you had it the whole time and it was just dormant. It is that place in your life that you need to look back at and say "Okay" and just do a little review.

Jen: *Hey Janelle.*

Janelle: Yes.

Jen: *We have about five minutes left and we've got a bunch more callers that wanted to get you. I don't want to cut you off. I thought it was a fantastic question, I thought it was fantastic in what she said because it's never come up before and I think probably, many people out there have the same issue.*

Janelle: Yeah, yeah. I totally agree.

Jen: *Let's go to the next caller because she has another question as well with how do you let your light shine when you have a lot of negativity at work and how do you bring spirit out in that capacity as well? So, we're going to...*

Janelle: Yeah, that's great. I would love to cover that. Yeah.

Jen: *Okay, you're on.*

Caller #3: Hi Janelle.

Janelle: Hey. Okay. So, with the work situation especially if you got a lot of drama going on and stuff like that, and it's extremely negative, this is somewhere where I have learned intensely, okay, because my husband and I started out our first business when we were 19, okay, and let's just say it is the polar opposite from what I actually do in the world, okay. So, I learned really early how to just shine no matter where I was and this is the mindset that I adopted. I let people experience the universe through me. And when you go in to that mindset and that thinking, you realize that there's nothing that can harm you or nothing that can distract you from being connected to your spirit. Because they're just wanting to be connected to who they are and they don't know how. And if you set the example, it changes something in their DNA.

Caller #3: Right. Are there times when there's too much negativity where you may need to sort of move on?

Janelle: Sometimes that is the case, yeah and that's about fine tuning that system, like that gut reaction I was talking about before, like is this a negative system? You know, do I not need to walk in the store? You know, that kind of thing. Sometimes that is the case. But for you, it is the earlier of the two.

Caller #3: Good reminder.

Janelle: Yeah, I know (laughs). But that's a great, great, great question and it's really about discerning what is best for you and I think we all know what's best for us and you know, we do. We really know.

Jen: *Okay, we have time for one more caller. I think we have a caller coming in from California and it just always happens with you, we're always down to no time.*

Janelle: I know (laughs).

Jen: *...call and so the caller with 310, we didn't have a chance to screen you, can you just ask Janelle your question?*

Caller#4: Hello.

Jen: *Yep, yep. That's you. You're on. Go ahead, go ahead with Janelle.*

Caller #4: Hi, is it me?

Jen: *Yes.*

Caller #4: Oh hi, good to hear you. I actually have a question. If you could give me any insight about my home living situation and making sure that I'm attracting the right environment, so that I can live fully in my spirit and also you know, shine into a new home in the way that I'm supposed to.

Janelle: Well, I think, with you, the trick is making sure that you don't go into emotions before you connect with what you need to do, you know, as far as like where do I need to live and that kind of thing. And then, especially when you're in a situation where you've got multiple people around that may not be connected in your living situation because that's supposed to be sacred space. You kind of have to teach yourself how to create sacred space where you are. And so, what that looks like is kind of taking a breath and really just asking your spirit to come fully in the moment and allowing this kind of bubble to form around you that people can come in and experience, but that does not detract from your energy.

Keith: *That is great advice. We're done in 45 seconds. I'm going to close this up with Jen. Janelle, I want to thank you for being our guest today, actually, Jen's guest, I'm just kind of doing technical stuff, but is there anything you're promoting right now or anything you want to let people know before we close? You've got about 30 seconds.*

Janelle: Oh yeah, yeah, yeah. My personal sessions, you can reach me at janellehoyland.com or you can find me on Facebook at Soul Healer Janelle Hoyland and I do group classes and online events and personal sessions as well and just love to serve the authentic self in you, and I just really am grateful to share this journey with you. So, thank you.

Jen: *All right, thanks Janelle.*

Janelle: All right, bye.

ꭨ Inside moments by Jen

Reading back through the transcript of this show, I realized that I cut off our discussion at a pivotal moment and asked to take calls. I didn't understand it at the time, but we had gone over so many new ideas for me and my vibration and energy were shifting in the very moment that we were discussing things. I reached a point where I couldn't take in what Janelle was telling me. This would happen at some point during each show. A lot of times, the theme would continue in the questions asked by callers. The main point of this show was for all of us to get back to connecting with who we truly are and that we stop looking to others to make us happy. We have the ability to look inward and reconnect with ourselves and our last call of the day was about how to anchor the spirit in the body. It is amazing the way Janelle and her Team worked with me to bring information through a caller if I couldn't get back to asking questions because the lines were so full or if I was "spiritually spent," meaning I took in as much spiritual information as I could for the show.

Show 1 – Soul vs. Spirit
Numerology perspective by Jen:
Life Path number 4

The life path number four is associated with hard work, determination, practicality and putting things in proper order. This reflects the message behind the show in that, to me, this show was a mini history lesson of who we are, where we've come from and what we are here to accomplish as souls on a journey. In some way, it is about work and about putting things in order and getting down to business to set the foundation to what your soul wants to create in this lifetime. It was also about Janelle and me working together and I think it also reflected our own determination to reach the masses and show people a new way to live and be in the world. I also hope we brought fun to the world of work because that's really what life is about. Work can be made fun and it can be a celebration.

Show 2 – Ushering in the Golden Age
Air Date: December 21, 2012
Life Path number 11/2

Jen: *We are talking about 12/21 and what that means. We are ushering in a new age, a new age of communicating with each other and being with each other.*

Janelle, could you talk about "the shift"? What is 12/21, what are we feeling, what does that mean to us?

Janelle: Right. Well, it's so interesting because, you know I have been talking a little bit about, you know, the energy kind of speeding up, speeding up, speeding up, and a lot of us can feel that ticking being faster, faster, faster, faster, but there is also a sense of agitation with it as well. So if you're a little more irritated with people or short with people, it's normal. The thing is, to you is, you know a lot of people look at it as the first thought, you know it might be the end of the world or apocalypse or some of those kind of odd things, but really in the Mayan calendar, it's just the end of the long calendar, which means it is the beginning of a new birth on the earth.

Keith: *Hey yeah. It's funny you said that, Janelle. It's funny you said that because I consider myself somebody with infinite amount of patience and when chaos is going on around me, I kind of just take a mental step back and just have a wonder about it all, but this past week or two, I have not suffered fools gladly at all and I have just had an infinite amount of impatience.*

Janelle: Yes, that is the shift. It's interesting because you could look at it, like "Okay I am being less patient or less compass- sionate," but it's actually that your spirit or your soul, it's kind of like in this little bit of frustration with the amount of negativity that we're experiencing on the earth and so we're kind of experiencing the negative energy, we're also experiencing the light as well. Well, so, you know I say, if I'm agitated and frustrated, that's a pretty good indication that we're having so much stuff going on because I'm extremely patient with people. And for me it occurs and I feel it from a deep place within me of "Come on everybody let's go, let's go, let's go," you know, we have somewhere to be, we have something to do. Quit complaining. Let's get there, let's get there, let's get there. Do whatever it is that you need to do, deal with your issues, be happy, do what it is, whatever it is, let's go. Let's collectively go, it's enough time we've wasted already, quit complaining and whatever the case may be. Let's go, let's open our hearts and express ourselves and go for what your desire is. What's your holding on?

Jen: *So is it your body catching up to your soul then? Is it the human reaction to everything, the subconscious, for some of us more conscious than others' reactions?*

Janelle: Yes.

Jen: *Has this shift ever happened before? Have we had little blips? (shifts) like this before?*

Janelle: Yes. Yes. We actually have, yes. In this lifetime as well as in some of the other past lifetimes as well. So, in this lifetime the blips happened in the week of 12/12. We had a little bit of frustration time in that as well and it is because the soul knows the truth, right? And it's always just going to be your unconscious leader to bring out the truth in you. And so, the world, you know, is moving there, right, a bit of a slow progression because we're dealing with, you know, phenomenon in the world that are extreme in nature and so the soul is having some sadness and agitation about that as well.

Jen: *Wow. So (we feel this in the body as) headaches, fogginess or, as you just said, agitation. How much longer are we going to be feeling this kind of thing? Are we not done with the shift? Does it ease up starting today or what happens moving forward?*

Janelle: Oh, that's a great question because it's something that was asked to me today. I'm not kidding you. I've gotten three personal phone calls from really good friends of mine this morning about that. And you know, and I wanted to know for myself so I already asked the question. I'm like okay, I know we shifted because I can feel it but when is the agitation or when is the headaches or when is the little bit of weight gain going to shift, you know that kind of thing and they gave me two days. They said the 27th and the 31st. But, I also know that there are waves of people. Okay, so like there is first wave of people, then the second wave of people, then the third, so that no one gets left out. Right of that we all consciously grow and evolve and experience the world in a different way.

That being said, I think the people that are experiencing those kind of phenomenon and the challenges within your body and emotions are—in your life as well—are what I call ground-breakers, first runners you know. And I think they usher in the way for other people to kind of jump on and I always say I get to do it first. So and then you know I can go, oh okay, yeah this is what that is (the agitation is related to the shift). But it's the waves of consciousness I feel like it does not mean you're any less connected or any less spiritual, or any less limited, you know it does not mean you are in a different place in your life. It just means that there are people that are going to help and—like myself in that transition, in that test.

Jen: *So, it's your soul—tell me if I got this right—your soul opening up to what you're put on the earth to do, right? And so as you awaken, you do the domino effect and awaken other people around you?*

Janelle: Yes. It's also not just what you're here to do but it's also who you are meant to be. Like who your soul is really. Because for the most part, you know kind of like I was saying last time, it's, you know, we're really touching 1% of our spiritual potential at any given moment. Because the body is built to work in conjunction with the soul, but the soul knows no time, knows no limits, knows no body in a sense. It knows only universal infinite space. So, putting it in a vehicle like the body, it's, you know, a little challenging when we have a big spiritual movement coming because the soul is just ready to go. It just wants to go. So, suppose your life, you know, like what kind of life you are meant to have, what your soul wanted to create in this lifetime. It has to deal with Karmic or life school and the other part of it is, what are you here to do, what you are here to give to the planet. What are you here to give to other people, your service? So...

Jen: *Ok, how do you get more in touch with that then? I know we're all awakening and opening up. Do you just keep tuning into your intuition and when it feels right you just sort of keep stepping in that direction? Taking what you're telling me on a macro level, how do we take it down to a micro level on a daily basis and apply that? How do we know we're heading in the right direction?*

Janelle: Well, I think that the one thing is some people look as if they are having frustration now, you know, like agitation and stuff like that. They look at that as "Oh well, then I'm not heading in the right direction" and sometimes that's not the case. Sometimes if you're experiencing those, you know, frustration or agitation moments, it's time to take a step out and say "Okay is this part of something else that doesn't have anything to do with me?" That's paying attention to your own surroundings and listening to your own intuition. But I think for most people, the quieter that you get, you know, within yourself, the more time that you take to nurture yourself, the more you will feel more inclined to live a life that is more authentic for who you actually are. And that looks like slowing down maybe. It's maybe, you know, maybe taking more runs or you know walking outside or whatever the case maybe.

Keith: *So, it's more about reaching a state of being rather than doing?*

Janelle: Yes. Yes. It's more—in my experience, you know in my own personal—you know because I also have to evolve through this process as well. It's not, you know, obviously when I was 15, I'm not connected in the same way as I was then, you know (my connection is) infinitely a greater experience now for me. And that came about by being in the moment with whatever that is that I need to be. So if I need to be present to my marriage, then I am more present to my marriage. If I need to be more present to my work, then I'm more present to my work. Whatever the case is.

Keith: *That actually makes a lot of sense. Because when you break it right down to the fundamentals, we are not humans doing, we are humans being.*

Janelle: Yes. Yeah, it's very true because that's what I said. You know the soul does not know what Earth Plane is or phenomena that we experience. That is a human body experience, so that is why there is frustration or agitation or body illness or things like that because you are bringing a large amount of spiritual remembrance in and the soul remembers, the soul knows that this is a limited capacity in the sense of the body. The truth is, is that there is no veil between this side and that. It's just a reality that either you experience or don't, and when you step into experiencing it, your soul will always lead you back to experiencing it which is being. It's not that it's for a select few. I think and believe that God intended it for every single person; that is how we were originally created, in this vehicle. There is just no possible way that we could experience this on a cellular level within our DNA if it wasn't encoded to be there.

Jen: *So, Janelle what's our potential then, you know, how you said we're using just 1%, right? What is the potential now? Can everybody just, if we all just step in, do we? What are they saying about that? How do we? How far can we go?*

Janelle: It's really unlimited. It is up to the body how much the body can take, you know because the—that's why we are experiencing challenges in the body right now, because, the body has to take a period of adjustment to bring in higher frequency. Because the body is really a dense vehicle, right, and so when you push and experience—not push, but when you—when we have a push universally and experience a lot of growth, you know. That's why some people can only experience it during near-death-experience, because it is a lot of energy to take in for the body. But the truth is, there is nothing that we aren't capable of doing. We are capable of healing ourselves, we are capable of not being limited by time. We are capable of experiencing our loved ones here as clearly as you and me. We are capable of interacting with angels and being led that way. We are, you know, capable of bi-locating and being in two different places at one time. All of these things I believe are natural talents that God gave us, but we were not ready for.

Jen: *Oh, we weren't ready for—okay. I was about to ask you what happened and you answered it. We talked about this last week; how we are born with the soft spot in our heads as babies and it is a direct channel. We have back and forth communication with the Universe and then it shuts down. So I was about to say to you, "Are we just continually blocking our connection with all of our stress from everyday life?"*

Janelle: Yes. And each moment that you connect like that very authentically, your body and your chemistry are not the same after these moments. You don't ever go backwards.

Jen: *Oh really? Is that right? Wow! Okay, wow.*

Janelle: You always move forward. Even though in appearances in the world phenomenon, it may be or in your thought process, that you are moving backwards, but the truth is, is that I have never seen or experienced anyone that is going backwards in our connection.

Jen: *I am heading off path for a minute but the question is parallel. How are children experiencing the shift? Are they going through it more easily or because they're getting all of our agitation and frustration, is it harder for them? Is there is anything that we need to do to help them?*

Janelle: Well I think, you know, the more grounded in our family unit that we can be, you know, the better for them. My kids are experiencing this, but I know in a sense, you know my kids are kind of like me, they're going to be a little bit ahead anyway. But when I ask them they say, you know, I do not know why I'm just frustrated and agitated. So not a lot from them. They say a little but you know they also say I don't really want to talk to you about that mumbo jumbo stuff. Well that's a teenager for you, so you know, in that sense. But, you know, getting back to the shifting part of it, you know that's why, you know, so many people are having so many things hit them all at once. You know, it's the losing the house, losing the job, marriages that may be struggling. It's your health that may be at issue, maybe your family is acting out more so than normal. All of those things. If you're getting hit with more than one, well you're in the shift, and that's okay. It will move. It just meant, you know, we're meant to learn something from it. Just like all of the experiences that we had. You know, going back even further to like 9/11 and then hurricane Sandy and then you know losing all the wonderful children (in Newtown, CT) that we did. Those are all heart-opening experiences. You know, because we need to know what really matters to us and I'm not making light of it at all, but just saying you know these are really big moments in our history when our kids read back on this to their kids. They are going to remember these moments as really big moments in history.

Jen: *Well, I think we said this, too, in heart-wrenching times, so many people come out to connect again and show support in so many different ways and everybody is uniting together.*

Janelle: Right. Which is what we're supposed to do.

Jen: *Yes, and I think it can be a huge wakeup call and many people say "Oh, my gosh, I just want to sit down with my sister, my mother, my child," and I just want to be. I just want to give them a hug. I guess your authentic self definitely comes through and it is still there.*

Janelle: Yeah, totally. And you know, it just is about the moments and the times that we're living in right now, are really about being very, very true to what is natural for us. It is natural for us to be compassionate and be giving of who we are. And almost, I would say, to the extent of giving what you have, you know, and giving what you're good at or giving, you know, in helping other people rise up from circumstances, you know. Not to say that there aren't people that are in the struggle and going to be in a struggle and no matter what, you cannot pull them out—that's also true, you know, because they have to have their own awakening. But we're not meant to be singular in our movements here. We are meant to move in groups and rally together and cheer each other on and experience that level of support and comfort in doing what we are here to do.

Keith: *Well, that's an interesting point, Janelle. What about those people who get through our lives living each day more as a lone wolf?*

Janelle: This is part of that. I know my brother-in-law is kind of somewhere in that instance. There is something within the minority of people that have that experience growing up. You know they weren't necessarily conditioned to be in group environments in the sense of being and feeling a "part of" or feeling, you know, aware of in that sense, and so it is part of your soul growth here to step out of that and to realize how much your vehicle can benefit from being in group support.

Keith: *It's interesting because, I must say, I actually have the experience of having people tell me they believe I'm extremely extroverted and extremely personable, but those interactions for me are very, very emotionally and spiritual draining and if I have a lot of them I find that I need at least that much individualized downtime so I can kind of internally spiritually recharge.*

Janelle: I do have a lot of people that experience that as well. Because there is a shift that needs to happen within your system that allows you to be of benefit to other people, but not at the cost of your own life. And so, it's almost that switch of the more you feed yourself the more that you can do. And, you know, knowing that when you take back your power in that sense; there is no one that can come into your experience that can take away from your energy or your light unless you allow it.

Jen: *That is such a good theme that just came up. You've actually said that quite a bit before, that the more you feed yourself, your world can become your Heaven on Earth.*

Janelle: Yes. Yes. That's what this time is about. It's about Heaven on Earth; that Heaven is not a place somewhere else, that it is here in front of you and it's up to you. It's up to you. Well, how much do you want to experience because there is no limit. There's no limit. There is no limit. There is no limit on finances, there is no limit on experiences, there is no limit on love, and there is no limit on health.

Jen: *I understand when you say that there is no limit, but how do you know you're heading in the right direction? I mean we talked about this, I keep asking you the same question, but I mean how do you know—okay there is no limit—how do you know when you're headed just on that right path so that everything does open up so you have the synchronicity, so you have the connections, those things sort of get easier, if you will?*

Janelle: Right. Well I'm hearing there are two processes. One is the head process and when I say head, I mean your mental process. Your mental process, right, will say "Do this, do more, do more, do more, be more, do more, do more, do more," right? That's not enough, not perfect enough, you have "to do more, say more, experience more, be more."

Jen: *Yes.*

Janelle: The internal, the heart intuition which is all about what we are coming into, is all about, "There is more than enough to go around and I don't have to drive my own train in a sense. I mean I do have to be ambitious," right? I do have to be ambitious. But it pings. It rings true. There's a peace in it that radiates through your body. And I don't care who the person is, right? You get advice from anyone. If it doesn't ping for you, if doesn't resonate, you know it immediately because you feel it in your body. You feel it. It's like truth; you know it when you hear it. There is just no mistaking it. It's absolutely clear. And the best way I can tell you is it pings, it radiates, it vibrates. It's solid, you can touch it, feel it, move it, know it, experience it.

Jen: *The ping for you, the stomach test, like it just, it sits right, or doesn't?*

Janelle: Yes, and that's how you know. That's your beacon. And the mind will try to analyze and make it fit. That's the issue. The mind will go "Let me make this fit because that's what so and so says." And this lifetime, this experience, this era that we're in is about how you become your own guru, your own best leader and not looking at an outside person as your leader or your guru or your mentor in that sense. Yes, we are meant to have mentors but we're also meant to find that within ourselves.

Jen: *Okay. Right.*

Janelle: So that's the "ping" thing. That's the "Does it ring true for me?" It doesn't matter what anyone else thinks: does it ping for me, does it ring true for me, does it feel like truth for me?... it cuts through everything else.

Jen: *Janelle, you personally don't have to ask yourself this question because you can already feel it; it's in you, right? So you can say yes, no or maybe?*

Janelle: Yes.

Jen: *But for the rest of us in a big decision or something we should be turning around and say "Wait a minute, let me check in. Let me see or..."*

41

Janelle: Yeah. Stop. Slow down. Don't just respond. In the world, I call it phenomenon because this is just a phenomenon experience, right? It is the reality, but it is not the full reality. It is just one slice of the pie. And this world is always about quick responses, quick responses first, you know, and they may not always be the right response. Sometimes it's a timing issue; sometimes it's a clarity issue. And it is sometimes taking a breath and saying "Okay, what feels right for me?"

What feels right versus what am I expected to do or be saying or you know. And sometimes it's about tuning, you know, tuning within and saying, "Okay, I'm going to let go of what other people are wanting me to do right now and just listen to what is true for me..."

Jen: *Okay.*

Janelle: ...with respect. You know.

▼ Inside moments about the show by Jen

We decided to take a call at this point during the show and the question the caller asked was directly related to our theme of Soul vs. Spirit and the Golden Age.

Janelle: Right. Yeah. Well, you've got like three questions into one, right? But this time, this is totally perfect. So here's the thing, there is the spirit, there is the soul, and they are two different faculties. Okay, the soul is the totality of all of your lives, all of your experiences, all of your emotions, every place that you've been, touched, felt, tasted, whatever and the combination of all the people, your family, your friends, your teachers, your connections. All of that is wrapped up in the soul. The spirit, however, is much like—and Jen and I had this conversation when I was there—is like the Holy Spirit, it's like drops of water. It is the movable, malleable, it almost is you can say intangible, also. In the same sense as the soul is, right? It knows no limits, no boundaries either, but the spirit also makes up your personality as well. And so, you will see your character traits show up in your spirit. Like for example, you know with Jen's spirit. She is very, you know, she likes to take in information and she is very chronological about things. You know, and she likes to have everything in a set order. That is her spirit, right? It's not being negative; it is just her spirit expressing itself. It likes to have that. It is enjoyable. But she also has this, you know, fun zany part. You know, that is her spirit. Her soul, right, is very spiritual, it has been here before, has done that, it has sometimes has very little tolerance for other people who don't necessarily get it exactly as she does. So, this is the beginning and I know Jen is okay with me saying this.

You can hear it in when she speaks. You can hear it. You can hear the different faculties when she speaks, you know, but like for myself, right? Example for myself is, okay, I am a fiery spirit, you know, I love mastering. I have a very playful young spirit, right, but my soul is a very old, wise soul who knows that everybody is going to get it, is comfortable with at what time frame they get it, you know, and it is not concerned about the timing of things. Sometimes to the detriment to other people— my timing sometimes is kind of all over the place because I know no time in a sense. So, that is myself. But then my spirit, what I was saying, it is very fiery. It lights up the room, passionate, you know spirit. It is just fire. It just loves to light and go. But how that affects, you know, the 2012 thing and the shifting, what it is that free will comes in the sense of, okay, well my ego might get a little irritated with how long it is taking to get somewhere. So I could opt for the free will category and say, "You know what, I'm done with it all" and rebel. My soul knows that that's not where the growth is. My spirit is very rebellious sometimes also, too. So there are two faculties in there. So how that plays out in this time frame, is that also that free will choices, the rebellious place of, you know, it is taking too long for me. I am pretty irritated right now.

⸷ Inside moments about the show by Jen

The next caller asked about the relationship between the spirit world and human experience and how they can work together.

Caller #2: I was curious about the connection between the spirit world and the human experience and how the two are working together with regard to 12/21/12.

Janelle: Yeah, it is interesting because for me, like, there has been an unprecedented amount of help in the sense of, like, when I connect, for me spiritually, like, always my vision is open, but I see so many more angels now and so many more guides and so many more teachers around people now. It is just unreal. And so it is a group project. It really is. It is not like we are lone rangers over here, as you know, just working our way to the battle zone and left without devices. They actually send us more help in times of growth.

Jen: *Let me ask you then Janelle, is that moving forward? Are they just going to stay around or then once we have all moved to the shift, are they going to sort of retreat back?*

Janelle: No, no. There is no backwards. It's actually more.

Jen: *Okay, so all the angels and all the helpers they are just going to keep staying with us to help us move on and move through?*

Janelle: Yes, yeah. The trick is you have to ask them. They don't intrude. They won't interrupt. They will protect us. But if you don't ask, they won't help. So you gotta ask. That is the trick and the other part of it is we get more and more and more and more help, the more we become spiritually open. It will become more and more and more and more as people become awake and aware. It is a ripple effect again in the spiritual world. It is just that we are meant to be supported. We are group beings in the sense of you know, we need support to do things. We need help. We are not meant to do things on our own.

Jen: *We've got about five minutes left. I don't know, Janelle, if you want to talk about anything else that you feel we need to know about 12/21, or the shift in the last couple of weeks of this year, or even in to 2013. What can we look forward to heading down towards January 2013?*

Janelle: Right. I think one of the things, you know, that you have heard me say repeatedly is to not hesitate on that which we are called to do and to be in our relationships. The other thing, too, that I find people experiencing now with relationship struggles in the sense of whether relationships are going to stay together or fall apart. A lot of people get afraid of change, especially in relationships, but that is important to know what is true for you in that sense as well, but I think you know, like, I said they gave me those two dates, the 27th and 31st as being important dates as far as feeling calmer, safer, more grounded in our journey here. You know, and myself knowing those dates for people, I think it is really important. You know they give you a focus point not necessarily to get there and like "Okay, this is the day," but more so just work on your being, and being in the moment, and being present to what you need to do for yourself as we go through and get closer to the end of the year. And this is our life school, you know. So don't get fixed on it as a reality, but just a piece of the version, a sliver, or whatever of what we are meant to touch and experience and be.

Show 2 – Ushering in the Golden Age
Numerological Perspective by Jen:
Life Path number 11

This show carried with it the life path number 11/2 so the combined energy of the master number 11 and the number 2. The traits associated with number 11 are intuition, connection to the subconscious, being a visionary, and with the number 2 are that of peacemaker, harmony and balance in relationships. The negative characteristics of both numbers are being too sensitive and avoiding confrontation. In this show Janelle talked about The Golden Age and that we are living in a time where the veil from this world to the Other is lifted. We have the ability to create anything we want and have access to anything we want at this time. Connection is key and our intuition is stronger than it has ever been before.

Show 3 – What Holds You Back From Starting Something New
Air Date: November 11, 2013
Life Path number 1

Jen: *Today we're going to be talking about new beginnings and the kinds of emotions that might come up around new beginnings. I know whenever I have a new project that I'm doing, something new, a new beginning, I one hundred percent go into fear mode, but the way it manifests for me is procrastination, kind of like walking in circles.*

Janelle, before we get to procrastination, I just want to ask you, we all went through this shift from 2012 into 2013 and a lot of us are still experiencing bumps in the road, if you will. Either somebody is sick or somebody's car breaks down or somebody loses a job. Significant things are popping up, and it's not like anybody expected a switch to go off and suddenly life would be fantastic, but I'm just wondering if you can give us a little bit of a temperature read of where we're at with this shift.

Janelle: Right. Well you know I think we all kind of do that. We're going to have this *moment* happen, and we kind of just wait for the moment, versus being in the journey part of it. I think we always tend to, as humans and people, we tend to look at the end result. We tend to wait for that, "When we burst into 2013, it's just going to magically change," without gauging the energy of what is required to experience that shift in awareness. The thing that I experienced yesterday; I had three of my clients who just got out of jail, who were extreme addicts. And they said they realized at the end of 2012 that it was time to make a significant change. And the very fact that they had never seen anyone or talked to anyone spiritual and they decided to do it this year is tremendous. Because we're talking about people who are really, really suffering, who broke out of that fear place and said, "You know what, there must be something else, because what I did isn't working." So I see that more often in this year than say last year. So that to me is a gauge for, if someone in that place is willing to look at growing in a different way.

Keith: *Do you see it as a veil being lifted? Is it awakening? How do you see it?*

Janelle: It's both things. It really is. The side between the veil or whatever you want to call it, or the place between this and that is thinner. But it's also this awakening that is happening *within* people.

Jen: *Sounds almost like breaking a mold. Or breaking a mold of who you were before. Or it's all about the preparation to do that. And as you're saying, this year we're all starting to step in. The light bulbs are going off in our heads to say, "Now is the time."*

Janelle: And you know, the thing is, too, there's waves of awakening. We can't obviously—well I guess we could, but we don't. We don't all awaken at the same time.

Keith: *I think it's difficult for those who are having an awakening or are walking in wakefulness to be interacting with those who are still sleepwalking.*

Janelle: Because it's a different conversation. You're having a conversation from the heart and from a vibration that is mutual. Like, "How can I serve you?" How can we do this together? How can we benefit other people? Instead of me, me, me, I, I, I, want,

want, want. It shifts into the collective energy which for a lot of people is not a comfortable space yet. So, yeah, it's a challenge in one way.

But the way I look at it is like, you know me, I love the challenge. I love to be like, "Yeah, let's go get it." I think that's why there are some people who are frontrunners in that sense. Because I don't really care in the sense of I don't care what I look like. I don't care what it appears to be. I don't care for the most part what I'm struggling with. Okay, it's a fear. Great, let's go. It's going to be there. You're human. You're always going to have some way, shape or form of fear in there, no matter what you're attempting to do, because you are a human. So I just maneuver around it. So this year I think we're going to have those little bumps, you know. And you can't have the bumps without the joy. Therefore, you realize what the joy is. So I think it's a good indicator of where you're at.

Jen: *How many bumps you have?*

Janelle: Yeah, let's look at the bumps. [laughs]

Keith: *It's almost like you have to be a phrenologist. The bumps are all in your head.*

Janelle: Exactly. It's just life in general. It's not meant to be smooth sailing in the sense of, "Woohoo, yeah, nothing is happening!" Really? Because you're operating around other people who have other things going on. We get to do that in Heaven. The objective is to collectively work on creating your own individual Heaven on Earth, which is what we're doing this year. And this is the lifetime and this is the space that we get to let go of all those karmic things from whatever lifetime, from

49

whatever family circumstances or things that you've put away, to go, "Okay, I'm not going to depend my happiness on what my circumstances are. I'm going to just move into happiness regardless of what shows up."

Completely. Because you're turning loose of the illusion that someone can create your happiness other than you.

Jen: *Okay. But let me just play Devil's Advocate here for a minute. In everyday life, when you bump up against some kind of challenge, either with family or friends, or life, how do you handle irritability? Because, for me, there always seems to be some sort of feeling of irritability when challenges come up. In my mind I am saying to myself, "Okay, there's a bigger thing out there." But, with everyday life challenges, getting through a morning with the kids, how do you get yourself back to connection? Or do you just shake it (the challenge) off?*

Janelle: Well I think the thing is we are all going to have some form or shape of irritability. It's that I see it. I have my own irritabilities or frustrations. It's that I look at them, believe me. It's the ability to look at those frustrations and say, "Okay, that's going to be there. I'm frustrated about this. That's going to be there for whatever time period it needs to be there." What do I need to look for within myself (to find) what is creating that? Or if it's the other person, "what is it I need to accept in them and just move into a place of harmony and balance?"

Because the soul itself, when you spend time with other people and when you're doing other things, is always going to try to find the balance in whatever relationship you're in. So it will constantly nudge you or move you towards what that love vibration is. So it's always going to want to bring harmony to whatever situation it is, whether it's you or the other person or the circumstance. So it's not the ability to let go of complete resentment and irritability because you're human. Things are going to trigger you. That's just a fact. And that's why I say it's not that I'm walking around just in constant prayer. No. I have kids. I have a family. They're teenagers. They have their things.

Keith: *I think you're almost on the right track. I don't think the soul seeks to move towards harmony. I think the soul is harmony.*

Janelle: That's a good analogy of it.

Keith: *One thing my mother used to say was, "We are spiritual beings having a human experience." I think the soul wants to replicate the otherworldly, ethereal heavenly experience here in our human sense. What do you think about it? Am I off or am I close?*

Janelle: I think we're having a technical difficulty right now, because the airwaves are breaking up for me. I'm only getting every other word. Just to let you know.

Keith: *I was basically saying that Janelle said, how did you phrase it? The soul seeks to be in harmony. And I said I don't think the soul seeks to be in harmony; the soul is harmony looking to take that harmony so we can have that in our human experience. I asked for your thoughts, whether that was close to being accurate or not.*

Janelle: Yeah, it's pretty close. The thing is that the soul has that composition of all the lifetimes. And so it's going to be relative to each person that you come in contact with. Because I believe that each person that comes into our lives, whether it's friendships or partnerships in the sense of business or marriage or family, whatever, is meant to enhance our soul's education. And it's not that the soul is limited in that sense. It's just it needs to bring to the conscious mind the awareness of what harmony is. And so the unconscious mind is always operating in that love/harmony field. The conscious mind is the one that we operate from, so the seed has to be planted or dropped into the conscious mind that you know, "Oh, that's requiring something different of me." Versus operating from the current program. It is that we are, on a greater level, at the seed of the soul, we are all conscious and aware and full of love and full of harmony and balance. And that's just how we were created. We were created in that likeness.

So I think, like I said, this year is more about more growth, more movement. We're going to see a little bit of bumps in this month, in January. But again, it's about bringing that harmony back and to realize that this is the playground. This is where we get to create. Life is where we get to create. It's meant to be enjoyed. And I think we lose track of that a lot.

Jen: *I agree. Especially when things don't go the way we want them to. Oftentimes, I go straight into that fear mode where I sort of pull back and I don't allow myself time to play. I get busy with the task at hand and then I completely cut myself off and forget my whole creative side because I'm not getting where I want to be. Then nobody has fun and nothing gets done.*

Janelle: Because you get irritable. Your spirit gets irritable. You just want to have freedom. That's the other thing, too, with children, they just have that natural free state. And as adults we say, "Ugh, I don't want to be that way. I'll just create what I want and it just flies off like a rocket ship," and all that kind of stuff.

Jen: *So what should we be asking ourselves when starting something new?*

Janelle: Well, I think it's interesting because the fear thing is really big right now because there are so many people on the heels of 2012 facing those really big life-changing moments, whether it's going into a new job, or whether it's ending a relationship or starting a family. Whatever those big life changing moments are, there's always going to be a bit of fear related to it, because it's the unknown. And we fear anything we don't know. But if you look at the unknown factors and say, "Okay, this is just a place of exploration." It's not that people, leaders or what have you, it's not that they don't have fear. It's they're courageous. They stand and look at that fear and move through it even though it might be frightening or it might be a little scary or apprehensive.

Each person that I have met, whatever kind of leader they are, they will always say it's not that you don't have any fear. It's that you see the fear and witness the fear and move with the fear to whatever goal you need to go to. And I think trusting yourself that you are always going to be led in the right direction is one of the main things. Because we get afraid that we're going to fall or mess it up or whatever the case may be.

If I told you how many times I have failed at stuff, well, not failed, but it didn't go the way I wanted to, whatever the case may be. The list would be not extensive, but it's pretty long; it's that I jump in all the time.

Keith: *You miss 100 percent of the shots you don't take.*

Janelle: Yes. You've got to jump and you've got to jump quick. And that's the other thing. That's how the universe works. It's a

53

very quick, fast-paced thing. You really don't get a lot of second shots at the same experience.

Jen: *So if your hand is up and you don't take the shot, they're going to move on to somebody else who is going to jump in?*

Janelle: Not necessarily all together. But in my experience, the things that I kind of hesitated on, sometimes it's a timing thing. But most of the time it's a fear thing. It didn't quite feel right, there was something amiss. I was hesitating myself. I didn't know if my family would be ready for that plunge. Because my Team has been wanting me to do a hundred gazillion things, and they forget I'm just Janelle. I have three kids and a husband and all that. I can only fit a little bit in my day.

Jen: *So fear should then be used as fuel, right? Let it fuel you. Use it as fuel to kind of spark you to say, "I'm going to jump ahead to whatever it is." Even though I don't feel quite like doing it, I'm going to take that first step and see what happens.*

Janelle: Right. Because it's not that everything you do when you face a fear is going to turn out a huge success. It's just about jumping in and facing that fear. My daughter asked me the other day. She's like, "Mom, don't you ever get nervous when you're about to teach a class or you're about to do a reading or whatever?" I'm like, "Yeah, I'm nervous and afraid pretty much most of the time." And I actually don't want that to go away.

Keith: *I used to do a lot of community theater and I can't tell you how many times I'd be waiting in the wings to go on and then like 15 seconds before I'm ready to walk onstage I'm forgetful of my* *lines and I panic. And then like five seconds before I have to go onstage, it all rushes back.*

Janelle: I think it's the universe's way of, I don't want to say keeping us humble, but keeping us very present to the experience. That's why I don't want it to go away. I like that. That shows me that I'm alive and I'm connected to what I'm doing.

Keith: *The fear is your adrenaline rush.*

Janelle: I asked my husband that, too, because he plays in a band and stuff. And he says the same thing, that right before he's going to play, he gets a huge "Oh my god!" freak-out moment. And no one knows that. No one knows that, except for him and I. I know it because I see it in him. That fear is there. Let it be there. Let it hang out. Don't let it stop you, unless it's meant to stop you. Like a fear for your life thing, that's a different thing. But in the case of going into new employment and going to search for a new job, I think this year is kind of interesting because I've got the questions of, "What is my purpose? Is that what I'm supposed to make a living doing?" And there's big confusion around that; I feel that people get confused with their purpose versus what they're meant to do for a living.

Keith: *Can you expand on that, Janelle? What's the difference between your purpose and what you're meant to do?*

Janelle: The buzzword has been around: "What's your purpose?" You need to know what God created you to do. You need to know that because it's a prime tool for operating in the world. But people make the confusion between my purpose means that's what I go make a living at doing. Sometimes the two are not

55

combined. Sometimes you need to go do work that isn't necessarily related to what your purpose is because God needs you to have fun so you can go do a bigger and greater purpose and not be defined or limited by making money doing that purpose.

Because the other thing I see is a lot of humanitarian things coming up in a lot of my readings this year. It's this overwhelming thing of humanitarian. And I think we're moving into that vibration on the planet more so. And so we need to understand this concept of, "I'm good at this. This is what God created me to do." That doesn't necessarily mean that's what you make a living at. Sometimes that's your hobby, that's your lifeline. It's what feeds your spirit, but it's not necessarily what you make a living at doing. Sometimes you're really good at something, say you're really good at computers, that's not necessarily what your purpose is. Your purpose could be that you feed the world.

Jen: *So I understand what you're saying, that you may run out and find something that pays the bills and then go be a photographer or something like that. But how do you know, "Okay, I found this. This is what feeds my soul"? How do you know when you've found your purpose? Is it all in the feeling? Is it different for everybody?*

Janelle: Well, I think for me, I think we come in with our purpose clearly identified and each one, no matter if it's two people and their purposes look similar, they're very different in what they are. I think the way that you'll know, one, is if you have a fear of survival in the sense of doing your purpose. So if you have a fear of survival and making money doing your purpose, that's how you know there's a bit of confusion in where you earn your money. That's why I'm a big advocate when people come to me and say, "I want to start this. I want to start that business," or whatever. I always believe in having the safety net. Because you will not feel safe or comfortable if it's something outside of what you're currently doing, if you don't have that thing to fall back on.

Jen: *That makes sense. You've got much more of an ease around you if your primary needs are met. You can pay your bills, you can feed your kids. And then you can be free to do other things. It's much more freeing to do what you want to do.*

⍦ Inside moments from the show by Jen

We paused to take a call at this time during the show. Our caller asked a question about forgiveness in relationships. I felt the topic of forgiveness applied to our discussion and so I continued that theme in the next part of the show.

Jen: *Janelle, how important is it, this sounds so elementary to ask, but it's got to be one of the things we need to do, for all of us out there looking for something new, is to forgive certain things that have happened, right? Can you just talk a little bit about that before we go on to the next caller? Because that's huge in how it came up.*

Janelle: Yeah. It's huge in the sense of all of our connections in life, whether it's family or work stuff or whatever the case may be, if there is any energy that is put out in the negative sense or anything we're holding onto, it can block us from receiving everything we're meant to receive. And the forgiveness part of it, and I know we've heard this a lot of times, is not for the other person. It's actually to free your own energy up so you can really be open to all avenues of something coming to you. And especially when it comes to love.

Jen: *How often do you see this, that when they come to you they've got someone who needs to be forgiven? How many times does it seem to come up for you that people are coming in and wanting something and you're seeing old ties, if you will, connected to somebody?*

Janelle: 90 percent. It's huge. It's a lot of wasted energy that I see. And I don't mean that in a negative sense. I just mean people aren't aware of how much energy they're expending in loose ends. The line completely broke up so I'm going to try to answer it.

Jen: *We're having technical issues today. It's a high-vibration energy. I swear that's why my phone rings. I'm telling you that is why the phones that I put on do not disturb, because of your energy. But I just asked, if you forgive somebody let's say one time from the heart, you put it out there that you want to release ties for yourself, for them, for the good of all. Can it come back to you? Can you own it all over again?*

Janelle: Here's the thing: can you have to revisit it? Yes. The thing is because we're multidimensional beings, right? And sometimes there are multiple lessons wrapped up in relationships. And you might go through levels of forgiveness or degrees or facets of forgiveness, let's say, towards yourself or towards the other person. And that's why sometimes it takes some time for revisiting that relationship and really understanding. The other thing I find that most people do, and I'd say that's about 90 percent, is they don't realize, and this is the missing piece in forgiveness: you don't realize the gift and the experience.

Jen: *The gift to sort of get out there and attract more that you want in?*

Janelle: The gift part of it is part of the lesson. "Thank you for this gift you gave me." That's part of the releasing that we do, to witness the person for whatever gift they gave to us in the form of a lesson or experience. But they taught you something wonderful about yourself. Whether they taught you to be stronger, more self-resilient, or more self-aware of internal dialogue, whatever the case may be.

But I think that's one of the key components: learning to witness the gift and the experience. That goes across the board, not just relationships.

Jen: *But you did get the positive out of the relationship, the gift. That's phenomenal.*

Janelle: So like I said, it's a lot of expended energy that you could be using to focus on other things.

Show 3 – What Holds You Back from Starting Something New
Numerology Perspective by Jen:
Life Path number 1

The title sums up the show completely in that we talked all about fear as that is what holds us back. I love that the date of the show added up to the Life Path number 1 because 1 is associated with new beginnings. I think the additional message was for all of us to surrender to our lessons and let down our guard so we can see and feel what is holding us back. Once we do that we can move forward to a new way of life like the one outlined in the first two shows.

The first section added together – Shows 1 to 3
Life Path number 7

When I added the Life Path Numbers of shows 1 to 3 and reduced the sum down to a single digit, I came up with the number 7. Life Path Number 7 is associated with bridging Heaven and Earth. For me one of the underlying messages of this section was to remind us that we are all connected. As we move into the Golden Age we are entering a new time to come together and share what we have with others. Share our unique gifts as they will better the whole.

CHAPTER TWO
SEX ON THE BEACH
RECEIVING AND INTIMACY

Show 4 – Protection
Show 5 – Receiving
Show 6 – Procrastination

Our first three shows were a success. We had a great time creating them and everyone who listened wanted to hear more. But instead of moving forward and planning more shows together, I did something over the next four months that I never thought I would do. I tested the Universe by procrastinating again. I didn't do this consciously but this behavior almost got me kicked off the show—not by Janelle, but by God Himself. I felt unworthy on the greater plan and so I got busy with everything else but the show.

During the months between shows three and four, my "to-do" list was packed. I became the "go to" person for everything from hosting play dates and school coffees to teaching Sunday school with my husband and helping out in the neighborhood if someone needed assistance with childcare or dog sitting. I was doing a lot, but nothing felt fulfilling, and our household felt the effects of my choices. Regular chores like laundry and meal planning were completed haphazardly, and I always felt like I was running from one activity to another with no time in between. Every time I turned around, I was cooking for some charity function that I was hosting or attending. I never felt that I gave 100 percent of my attention to Dee or the kids during that time. Instead, I felt like I cooked my best meals for other people or listened most intently to people outside my own home. I told myself I was being productive and that I was doing good things for others, but I had a feeling of restlessness in the pit of my stomach all the time because I knew I had greater work to do for myself, and I was putting it off. Deep down, I knew I was losing out, but the fear of living full out and being my authentic self still scared me. I repeated the same pattern I did before we launched the show: Instead of looking inside myself to find the reason for my procrastination, I again looked to other people. In reality, the show was part of my purpose and soul work, and it already served others, but I felt unworthy of that greater plan. So I denied myself (and everyone else) the experience of the show for a few months.

What I learned from the next three shows

When Janelle and I agreed to broadcast a show about protection, I thought we were going to talk about how to be safe in the energy realm. We did talk about that but halfway through the show Janelle shared that protection is also related to speaking your truth. Your truth isn't just about being honest; your truth is also *believing* and *honoring* the fact that you are a Divine Being with unlimited access to anything you need. You don't need to *become* worthy of anything; you already are worthy just by being your true self in as many relationships as you can throughout your lifetime.

What I learned from the show was that honoring my Divine truth starts with being completely honest with myself first and then with the people around me. When we aren't honest with ourselves, we deny our greater truth and that limits our ability to receive new gifts and experiences from the Universe. I didn't set out to "people please" as much as I always had. Oftentimes, friends and acquaintances would catch me on the go and ask me to help out with something while I was in the middle of school pickup, or at the grocery store, or just running errands. I would say yes without even pausing to think about what I had on my calendar already or if I even *wanted* to do the task at hand. There were many things I really wanted to help with, but there were also many that I just didn't have time for, or I wasn't a good fit for the task, so I never should have said yes in the first place. I didn't think saying yes when I really wanted to say no would affect my life in such a powerful way. For example, I thought helping with one garage sale when I really didn't have time wouldn't throw off my soul work at all. I was wrong. I ended up putting my own goals on hold and the other party suffered too because someone else may have done a better job than I did, but they never had the chance to find out because I had already taken on the project. I also thought even if I wasn't being 100 percent honest when I agreed to do things for other people that I wouldn't affect everything else in my life. I was wrong on that front, too.

In order to overcome this, I first had to come out of denial and look at what I was doing. I had to review my calendar and really see how over booked I was and *feel* the effect it had on me and my family. For two to three weeks, I just observed the schedule and felt the effects on my energy and the vibration of the house. It was extremely painful for me to see how many times I put off playing with my kids, spending time with my husband, or doing something for myself because I had so many outside commitments. All I wanted to do was take everything off my plate so I could establish a feeling of calm around the house, but I needed to finish what I started and keep my commitments. It was more beneficial for me to live with the energy-vibration of over scheduling so I wouldn't do it again.

Breaking my pattern of people pleasing was not an easy process for me at first. I found it hard to say no to people in the beginning, but once I started really checking in with myself, I could easily feel how my body reacted to what I was being asked to do. When I got a feeling of heaviness and agitation in my stomach, I knew what I was being asked to do wasn't in alignment with where I needed to spend my time. I also knew that there would be an answer to the other person's need from someone else. I learned to be honest with myself and allow myself to be vulnerable enough to say no and to be okay with the other person's reaction. Being myself and speaking my truth benefits everyone. I've learned saying no to someone gives them the opportunity to speak *their* own truth, to take responsibility for what *they* are here to do and learn their own lessons in the process. By saying yes when I should have said no, I may have blocked a connection from someone else that they needed to make.

I've learned that Divine Guidance serves as protection. God is always trying to connect me to people, events, and opportunities that will help me accomplish my soul work and have fun while doing it. When I follow my intuition and check in to see if something feels right, I'm not just checking in with myself, I'm actually checking in with God. The trick for me is to allow myself to surrender and let myself be led by God and *not* by my friends or the outside source asking the favor. That takes courage because I can't see the final result, but I have to trust that taking the next step in the direction they are leading me toward is for my highest good and that my life will get easier if I follow that guidance. I have to trust that God knows the bigger picture better than I do. Trusting Divine guidance and saying no to a request when it doesn't feel right, is protection, protection in terms of freeing up my time and protection in terms of keeping me on track to accomplish my purpose: soul work and opening myself up to receiving more gifts and connections from the Universe. Saying no to someone else is saying yes to my Divine Plan and reinforcing my truth.

Funny Moments by Janelle

On this show there was not a live audience, which truly showed how much we have to learn around intention. We had a grand time bringing these shows on air, although all three did not have a live audience. We laughed, knowing that this was a sign of where we were with intention. It was totally obvious that this was a very clear lesson for all. We spent almost an hour laughing at the thought. We had to set the intention live that this would anchor, set the stage for people to enjoy all three of these shows for a long time after the initial airing of them. It was a great opportunity to trust faithfully that while not one person was live with us, it was still amazing information. Talk about the universe playing with us.

Show 4 – Protection
Air Date: June 21, 2013
Life Path number 6

Jen: *Today we're going to be talking about protection. Janelle, before we do that, I am wondering if you can talk a little bit about what I would call the heartbeat of the Universe and what's going on for people today and what you're seeing around us at this time.*

Janelle: Absolutely. Well, you know, we're in these interesting fluctuations both in May and really the whole month of June. May hit us with a good dozy. I know most of my personal life was kind of affected with that. We have two lunar eclipses. We were sandwiched with those, and in the middle of the solar eclipse, and then now as we go into facing June, we're having a super moon this weekend, which sheds light on things that we're struggling with, things that we need work on. As we know, the full moon kind of makes us extra sensitive emotionally. All of those things coming up, but I also just intuitively kind of feel like this, I don't know, for myself, it feels like a little constricted energy or a little tight, tightness. Like something's about to manifest or occur.

Jen: *You mean like a positive thing for all of us? I do agree with what you said. I feel like May, for me was just crazy. I remember texting you one day saying, "Hey a little bit of help here. What is going on?" Did you mean we all had a push though? We're all going to feel a little bit more relief? Do you have any idea how it's going to manifest itself?*

Janelle: I think with, like I said, May being okay we got hit with numerous, various different things at one time, and going into June. June being the time when we have to look at those things that we went through in May and figure out, "Where am I blocking myself off? What am I restricting myself with?" At the end of June going into July we get relief from July through August. It's a good thing. It's just meaning, okay sit down and take inventory of where are you wanting to be and what are you holding yourself back on?

♈ Inside moments about the show by Jen

During this show we decided to take a call before we started to talk about the topic of protection and once again the call was completely related to our topic. The caller had a question about her relationship, but Janelle channeled in the theme of speaking your truth in relationships and that ended up providing a perfect introduction for our topic of protection. The timing and questions of our callers always amazed me because their questions were always connected to the theme of the show. They were inspired by Divine Timing.

Jen: *Janelle, that seems to come up all the time. Speaking your truth seems to be huge in relationships. Can you just speak a little bit more about that?*

Janelle: It's one of the things, relationships is one of our learning curves in this lifetime; it's learning how to navigate around someone else while remaining connected around our authentic self. That's why when I'm reading for someone and I feel like they are diminishing their light in some way shape or form in order to serve another, it is not what we're supposed to be doing. Speaking the truth means, okay, if you're having a conversation with your significant other, partner, friend, whatever, it doesn't matter. Whatever source of relationship it is, you're meant to stand in a place of honoring who you are and speaking whole heartedly from the place of truth. The place of truth may not be what your opinion is.

Jen: *That's a key piece. (may not be what your opinion is)*

Janelle: It may be that there's something in you that is causing whatever lesser feeling within yourself. Your opinion may not be serving the whole. Sometimes they think to get a second opinion versus what the truth actually is.

Jen: *How often does this come up? I know you talk to married couples and people in relationships. Does this just cycle through? If you're together with somebody for 50 years, is it a cycle? I am speaking my truth for who I am today, but who I am in five years may be different. Is it a lesson all the way through?*

Janelle: Yes, yes, it is. It is. You do vibrationally change as you grow, as you learn more about yourself, but the goal is to enjoy the experience as a whole experience while remaining truthful to who you are in the moment. The same is said for the other person, whether it's your sister, mom, dad, your husband, your wife, whatever, your children. It's all about maintaining that connection to yourself while serving the greater good. That may make you feel uncomfortable at times. It may not be what you think it is as far as your opinion. You think the other person should change. That may not be what they're meant to do in this life. You may be moving that person. The nature of relationships themselves, has to flow just like we have flow with the universe. There will be times of constriction where the other person is really fine and we are floundering around a little bit, and we're fine but our partner may be floundering along a little bit. That's the nature of relationships themselves is just to know that and stay consistent. One other thing that they just brought in, it's also the same for you and the Universe.

Jen: *Wait. Hold on. It's also the same for you first and the Universe?*

Janelle: Yes, they related it to, what they said to me, is the same relationship as if you were like married or you have family, whatever. We are connected to the universe and to God or light or source energy has flow in it, too.

Jen: *If I'm not speaking my truth in my marriage or my friendships, I'm probably not speaking my truth as I am to the Universe or God. Is that what you mean?*

Janelle: Yes.

Jen: *Got it. People speak your truth. You're kind of muddy here; you're going to be muddy up here, too.*

Janelle: To understand that doesn't make you diminish in how well you're connected.

Jen: *Just what you're going through at the time.*

Janelle: What you're doing at the time. They understand that better than we do.

Jen: *Okay.*

Janelle: We're the ones that have freak outs.

Jen: *Who Me? No. never, ha ha. Ok, moving on to our topic of Protection. Can you tell us what protection is, how it fits in with all of us and where we are individually, universally, what we all need to do to be protected?*

Janelle: I think as we all are consciously aware, there are Earth changes happening. There are changes within our lives occurring. There's also, what I've experienced, a little bit, there's a lot of judgment going around. People form their opinions left and right about people without thinking. I've also seen within my own life and also experienced with other people in sessions and what I was talking before about with the dream state, even for myself. I've experienced really strong fear-based dreams that are not normal for me. It's not normal for me to wake up and have a fear dream happening. When I ask a question to the Universe—because I always do that—what is this about? What's occurring? What do I need to know? They said that you're experiencing times with extreme light and dark. It's not our personal battle, but we get caught in the energy. It affects us. That's why we sometimes feel gloomy, like I said before, concentrated energy or we feel disconnected. Whereas before when you go into meditation and get a quick answer and now you don't. All of those things are because we're experiencing heightened times of awareness, but I do know that it's about us moving through those places and becoming more connected to who we were originally created to be.

What occurred to me was we needed more protection. Because this isn't our battle, and what I mean by that is, when I see my dreams occurring that way, there's this alternate awareness about me that says, "I know that's not my battle." If I go into this, just with myself, with fear whether it's about work or relationships or whatever, if I deal with those dreams, and I own them as mine and they become mine and the dream from the experience. If I wake up in the morning, and I go and that was the battle of light and dark. It has nothing to do with me. It is actually the spiritual warfare that's being battled in ways for me, that's a whole different vibration. We need protection because when we sleep at night we travel. Our spirit, I don't care who you are, if you're on this planet, you may or may not be aware of it, most people are. We travel. We leave our bodies; we go connect to whomever we had a conversation with in the day. We go see our ancestors. We go just rejuvenate our bodies or whatever the case may we. We always travel; it's not a question. We do that, we leave our bodies open. What I understood is we just really need to understand we have to ask for more protection than we normally would have. I don't mean that to scare anyone, but you can see it in reality. You can see it on the news. You can see it in conversation. People are more agitated. They are quick to jump. We're living in the most amazing time in that, also. To look at one thing and say, "Oh this is doom and gloom." NO, it's actually the opposite. We're living in the most; we're forging ground for everyone else after us. We're the ground breakers. We get the extreme versions of everything. Everyone else that comes after us, children, children's children, they're not going to have to deal with what we had to deal with because we said, we wanted it. In that means you need to understand and ask for full out protection during these times.

Jen: *Okay. What I think is amazing, Janelle, you say the majority of people know that they do astral travel; that they leave their bodies and they have some kind of memory of it. For those people who are hearing this for the first time and don't understand that* *when we go to bed, our spirit leaves, we go places. What do we have to do then to protect ourselves in that place?*

Janelle: I really say, for me, one of the things that is not a question is, I unconditionally just pray and say "May you surround me as I sleep, protect me as I rest, protect me as I journey." To say, I'm just going to pray when I wake up in the morning, that's fine, but the times that we're getting inflicted is between three to six a.m. When you travel out of your body, the feeling is, when you wake up in the morning and you're groggy, you don't have your footwork yet because your spirit isn't all the way in yet. Before you hit the ground, your spirit is still a little bit out of your body. That's why you're kind of groggy. Even if you hit the floor sometimes it may take a little bit. That's also how you know you're spiritually connected, also. In the sense that you wake up groggy so you know you've left.

Jen: *Is there a night when we just don't want to astral travel?*

Janelle: We're always either recharging or connecting. Either one.

Jen: *Otherwise, how the heck would we survive down here if we can't give ourselves a break?*

Janelle: The thing is, we're not just this body. We're not just this earthly plane. We're not this spirit. The way they explained it to me is, we are at least 10,000 eons of time.

Jen: *Wow.*

Janelle: That's huge. How could you limit yourself into this one body? All the time. That's what I mean when I'm saying speak your truth. Your truth is that your awareness, your consciousness at any given moment can access anything that you're wanting to have or needing to have in this lifetime. There's nothing standing in your way. There's nothing to mend, heal, fix, correct. When you stand in that truth, you change your vibration enough that you can be in the place of total vibrational match for that which you are seeking. The protection part of it is protecting your whole being in all states.

Jen: *You can step in and connect with whatever it is you need connecting with.*

Janelle: To think you can walk around in the world without protection right now, that's why we needed to have the conversation is because there, to say there's not a battle occurring, okay. Watch the news. Listen to how people speak to each other. Watch what's occurring, and then you'll understand there's a warfare happening, and it's a warfare for our souls.

We have to align together. The more that we come together in prayer and love and positive and energy and wanting everyone to get to where they need to be, the more that we raise ourselves out of that place and it can't affect us.

Jen: *You always say such profound things that take my mind just a few seconds, like okay...even though I'm on air, I'm like wait a minute.*

Janelle: You should see me on the other side of it. You think I'm consciously aware of what I'm saying. Did I just say that?

Jen: *You are saying, we just have to live in the moment and live and know we have access to all. I always feel like I get stuck in* *everyday moments. I have to ask myself how do I get that accessible role again? What do I do?*

Janelle: It works like this. Before you go to bed at night, ask that you be protected while you travel. Ask that your loved ones be protected while they travel. That you wake up in the morning fully connected to who you are, which is just love.

Jen: *Yup. Got it. Okay.*

Janelle: Ask that you operate from that place.

Jen: *Janelle, do you just want to continue for a few more minutes on what more we need to know about protection? Also, can you tell people a little bit of what we have in store in the future, what's trending for all of us in the Universe?*

Janelle: One of the things I was telling you about, protection, and making sure we surround everyone in our lives, not just ourselves, but everyone. We extend that out. We extend that bubble out. One of the conversations that I had was, and the reason I just taught the class on Protection is, that I recently became aware in my consciousness I do something different than most people do. I don't diffuse things, I don't do crystals. I don't just pray. I actually become protection. I needed to understand how I can teach that to people. What was occurring in the world was that we need to understand how to become that. It was about trust. What I got was that I, without a shadow of a doubt, I trust 100% in the universe and God and whatever you want to call it. There's no question for me. I become solid in that. That's what you feel when you come in with me or in conversation with me is, it's solid. It's a bubble. You go into an alternate reality. It's solid. It's not an amoeba effect. It's this or that, Yes or No. There's no in between with me. That's what people need to understand is, they need to become solid in who they are. Solid in their protection. Solid in their conviction. Solid in their love for themselves. Solid in what they have in people for their life.

Jen: *Do we have to become solid in we are first to kind of get ourselves to where you (Janelle) are?*

Janelle: Yes.

Jen: *Because I've stood next to you. I've experienced the bubble, and it truly is a completely different experience to stand next to you in a room than it is with anybody else that I know. It's amazing to me it always comes back to ourselves; again it's speak your truth. Be who you are.*

Janelle: That's why we were waiting for the 2012 thing. We have that happen, and had all these things like the peripheral speed bumps. We had how many of those? We are like, "We finished 2012, yay!" Then we are like "what happened", 2013, we are still having bumps in the road. Major bumps. I asked the question because me, I'm like okay…I just go straight to the Universe and say "Tell me what this is about. Tell me this. Tell me that." So I can understand and know what it relates to. Tell me what it relates to. As we go through the purging and releasing of our identity. I'm separate from you. You're different from me, and to realize that we all innately have the same connection, which is love or intuition or whatever. The same light, air, the same breath, we all share that energy. To think that people aren't coming into your experience, to think they're coming in for no reason, you're putting blinders on. Every single person that comes into your conversation, into your life is serving a purpose. Your job is to be open to that purpose.

Jen: *And understand you're completely protected?*

Janelle: Yes.

Jen: *In that moment. In all moments.*

Janelle: Nothing is coming into your experience that is not meant for your good. That's what the trust is that I have.

Jen: *That's the key piece that I think I have to understand. It's all for your good even though it doesn't always seem that way as you're walking through it in all the things that happen.*

Janelle: It's always, always, always just moving you to that place of the next vibrational place that you need to be at and to move and to move and to move and to move and to constantly be evolving and shifting into that appreciation of the fact that you have to change a dirty diaper or you have to have a conversation that you don't want to have.

Jen: *It's almost like we have to do another show on that. All of our experiences are all for our good because as we say, when you're in the middle of a dirty diaper or the car issues or what have you, whatever, you forget. It goes right out the window. What do you mean it's for my own good?*

Janelle: Right, the experience with my car catching on fire. I'm driving down the freeway, and I have that moment of "Holy crap what's going on?" Then I relaxed. I am going to get where I need to go. It's fine. It's going to happen the way it needs to happen.

The tow truck driver told me how I had an angel standing with me. What? That's because I was open in the initial part of the journey.

Jen: *Janelle, we've got two minutes left. How do we move on from here? What do you see? Do you see anything as I said, trending, moving forward? We know what May and June was. You said July is kind of a break, not a break...a coast if you will.*

Janelle: It's like a coast. Like a neutral. One of the things I know without a doubt is we're supposed to be working on those things that we put off that we have to get going, but we also need to move. We need to move quicker and find time for ourselves too. July, August and September are really about taking action and going after what it is that we want or what's going to make our heart sing or what's going to make you happy. Not at the cost of you, and not the cost of someone else, but working that into the original plan.

Jen: *Okay.*

Janelle: You always have to serve the other people, too.

Show 4 – Protection
Numerology perspective by Jen:
Life Path number 6

We continued on the vibration of a 6 into this show on Protection. Again, the traits associated with the number 6 are home and family, nurturer and teacher. In this show, we learned that protection is about trust and trust that the Universe has your best interest in mind.

Show 5 – Receiving
Air Date: June 28, 2013
Life Path number 4

Jen: *Today we're talking about receiving and what that means. Janelle, I'm going to turn it on over to you and just ask you what does receiving mean to you, and what do you think it should mean for all of us?*

Janelle: I think, just in my experience in my own life, I had to learn the lesson of how open was I to receiving help either through people or through the universe. I think that's what receiving is.

A lot of times, we ask the question, "Why am I struggling through this?" or "Why am I not having support?" whether it be physical support or Universal support. We kind of throw our hands up in the air and go, "Ugh," and we feel overwhelmed, you know.

Through my experience just looking at the times where I have asked that question, you know, "Why do I feel alone in this?" or "Why do I feel not supported in this?" or "Why am I struggling through this?" or "Why is there not help?" was because I was blocking something. Whether it be open to guidance through other people or from the universe, through meditation, whatever or physical support like someone offering me something, did I block that? Or did I say, "Yes, thank you, more please." I think we're kind of trained to be really independent, to not ask for help a lot.

We're taught from a very young age. We do that with our kids, (we say) "Do it yourself." Then we forget that we need to teach ourselves as well as our children how to ask for assistance and be open to receiving help.

Jen: *Okay. It's funny, I was about to ask you that question. I was about to say why do you think—first of all, do you feel like a lot of your clients struggle with this issue? Is this something you see comes up time and time again?*

Janelle: Yes.

Jen: *And is it simply because, like you just said, for whatever reason culturally, it seems we are all taught to be independent and not rely on one another? I was going to say what makes us block out our own ability to receive? Because I have a feeling if you were to ask somebody if they're a good receiver, probably the majority would say, "Oh yes, I'm good at that. I get stuff all the time."*

Janelle: It's so true, yes. It's definitely that case. Not only is it something that we're taught, but it's also in the sense of when we pray and we ask for something; we don't ask for help in order to get where we're going. We just ask that the problem be fixed.

Jen: *Right, we just ask for the thing that we want (the problem to be fixed).*

Janelle: Yes, we don't ask for the tools to help us get to where we want to be or the guidance. We don't ask for the guidance in order to be clear in the moment about what we need to receive. Yes, really, truth be known, even myself as good as I am at receiving, even I ask for assistance, being more open to receiving.

Jen: *Okay. Can you give us some examples maybe if any come to light from some of the themes that you've heard from your* clients? Like, for example, what would it be like in a day for somebody who was open to receiving versus somebody who wasn't? How do we all break it down so that we can allow ourselves to be more open? Or what are some examples from clients that you may be able to think that were struggling? Just to teach our listeners how to go about learning how to be more open?

Janelle: One of the things really clearly is like I said, the praying and asking for—we just ask that the thing be healed or show up. We just pray for the end result. We don't pray for tools or assistance in understanding what our next step is.

Jen: *Oh, that's huge.*

Janelle: Because we're always, always, even myself, we're focused on the end result. Really, when we look back, it's the journey that we're most proud of. One of the ways that I would say is a huge thing is being open to what is my next step and asking for help with what that next step is, so literally saying out loud, "Please help me be open to what my next step is."

Jen: *Right, and that actually kind of centers on what you said last week. Correct me if I'm wrong. I know we had a caller who was having difficulty setting boundaries between work and home. I think on the show you had said we're really only good at doing one thing at a time. I almost feel like this bridges the gap from last week in sort of saying, "Okay, what is my next step? How do I get to the next step? How do I get there?" What is that message like when it comes through? I know it's going to be different for everybody, but what is it like to receive that next message?*

How will we know when we've received the help with the next thing and how do we keep ourselves from shutting ourselves off to receiving, if that makes any sense to you?

Janelle: No, totally. (Yes, it makes sense). Yes, one of the things I think most people assume that I just sit in meditation all day. That's just my life, genie in the bottle kind of moment. No. I have three kids. I have a ton of stuff going on at any given moment if you really sit down and ask me.

One of the things is that I'm so open and so clear about conversations. The thing is, the messages about your next step could come through the grocery store clerk. It could come through a TV commercial. It could come through an Internet ad. It could come through a magazine article. It could come through the dog running down the street.

Jen: *I love that.*

Janelle: The thing is you don't know at what point is the message going to be delivered to you about what you need to do. Your job is to be open and receptive to—the Universe is going to use everything and anything. Once you throw open that field and you say, "I'm open to what my next step is," your job is to really be open and perceptive to what your outside world is doing.

Jen: *Okay. If you don't get it the first time, which probably a lot of people don't—are they just going to keep pushing through? Like, "Here it is" thrown out to you for the eighteenth time? Or, like me, if I don't get it then Janelle calls me and says "Hey, your Team is trying to get through to you?"*

Janelle: Yes, so true. They'll hit you over the head with it, yes. It's just that we are trained not to ask. I can't tell you how many times I go into session with someone and they say, "We can ask?"

Jen: *Right.*

Janelle: We can really ask for? Yes. What do you think? They want to help you. They want to, but they're not allowed to intervene unless you ask.

Jen: *What should we be asking for? Every single thing? The big things? The little things? For example, my kids and I play the game about parking spaces. Let's see if we can get a parking space (up close). For example, for you Janelle, how many different things do you ask for? For yourself or even with a client or in the day in the life of someone who is open to receiving, how many different things do you ask for? I know each day is different, but on a daily given basis, or even with some of your clients that you've seen over the years, have we gotten better with receiving?*

Can you give some examples of ways they have turned it around?

Janelle: I think one of the biggest ones, a good example, yesterday I had a client come in. She had been struggling with love and relationship, and really had a lot of guilt around her personal decisions in and around relationship. One of the things we got to was that, ultimately, she felt unworthy of love. One of the biggest blocks that I see is that in receiving is at the core of it, we don't feel like we're worthy of receiving help or good things. It's not that we walk around in this bubble that says, "I'm unworthy." It's an unconscious program that we have that we feel unworthy or guilty. Moving out of that paradigm into stepping into love and harmony with yourself, knowing that, okay, you're not going to get it perfect every time. You're going to stumble. You're going to fall, but ultimately it's about freeing that guilt up and stepping into worthiness and alignment with receiving. When we had the conversation yesterday, moving her to a right place with relationship, meaning we had the conversation about how often does she let a man help her with anything, from carrying the groceries to opening a door, to asking for assistance at work from a coworker that happens to be male.

Whatever the case may be, how open was she to male assistance physically because she had some sort of guilt around love? We worked on that and she understood that that was her needing to prove to herself, "See, I'm unworthy. I'm unworthy of relationships. I'm unworthy of male support in my life."

Jen: *Okay, wow, that's phenomenal. Keith and I are going to take a musical break but I want to ask you when someone feels unworthy does it matter if you find out where the core of that is coming from or do you just simply need to make a different choice when you move ahead. Don't answer that yet. I want to ask when we come back. We are going to take a quick break now.*

❦ Inside moments from the show by Jen

The message and energy of this show was so powerful for me I had to take several musical breaks to comprehend what Janelle was bringing across. This is a moment in the show when I stopped Janelle in the middle of a key point.

Jen: *Janelle, does it matter if we know where that feeling (of guilt) may come from or do we just simply have to change how we approach things?*

Janelle: Well, it's definitely true that it really doesn't matter what the object was that created the unworthy feelings because I believe that in general, we kind of come in with a little bit of that disconnect from the universe which causes the unworthiness feeling. It is part of our process in this lifetime to move into abundance with that and discover that we are ultimately worthy of everything that we truly desire. It is all available to us. So, in a sense, it really doesn't matter where it comes from because you can go into the deepest places of your spirit, your soul and you'll find any number of places where the unworthiness theme shows up. But it is exactly that. It's a personal decision.

In my own life, I could have any number of reasons that I can sit here and say, "I'm unworthy," but I don't operate in that space. That's a personal choice. It's a personal choice, a personal decision to move into abundance in alignment with what you need to receive from the universe and how quickly can you get there.

Jen: *For you or anyone else then to get that shift to happen, do you have to ask for help or ask yourself what am I thinking? Am I slipping into being unworthy? What's my next step? Then remember to ask for help for that next step.*

Janelle: Right.

Jen: *If like attracts like and, let's say, I'm someone who struggles with worthiness, on the whole, am I going to be consciously or unconsciously surrounding myself with people who also struggle with that or are we all at different areas and different days, etcetera, and so on? How does that work?*

Janelle: You know, I think we kind of do an ebb and flow with that also. We, at certain moments, attract people in that we need to reflect worthiness to, and we attract people that are emanating worthiness to us.

It is a give and a take system. We are always conspiring to either reflect or be reflected to. It's either to be reminded or to be the reminder. If you understand that, then when you see someone who is not operating or someone comes into your experience that isn't working in worthiness or understanding their worthiness, or the facets of being open to receiving help, or receiving gifts or blessing from the universe, it's our job to be consistent with that in that place and not shift out of that.

If we do shift out of it, to quickly see it and come back into balance with it, people get sent to us to help us, remind us where we're not doing that. Then we are also sent to people to help them understand why they are not. Whether they're conscious of it or not or whether we're conscious of it or not doesn't matter.

It's a feeling within you, whether you feel off-center or in balance.

Jen: *What if you're with someone and they're just not getting that lesson? Let's say you're sent to them to help them figure out they're worthy, and they are constantly just not getting it? For example, my girlfriend is going through a situation where she's just not able to receive, feels uncomfortable receiving gifts of any kind. For whatever reason, it's just not something that she's comfortable with. How do you help? Are you just simply the role model?*

Janelle: Yes, exactly. The thing is that a lot of people get confused in the sense of, we think that we need to go help them or enlighten them or help improve their world in some way, and that's why we're having the epiphany in the moment, that they're not getting it. Really, it's more about honoring the place that the person is in while seeing what their potential is, so holding the vision for them of moving through this, but allowing them to be where they're at and demonstrating, "Okay."

Really a long time ago it was explained to me by my Team—and this will sum up receiving in a nutshell completely—when you understand that the person that's bringing you XYZ, doesn't matter if it's a thing, if it's a message, if it's a hug, whatever, when you understand that that is really the Universe or God moving through that person to bring you something, and the act of denying that gift from whoever is giving to you is denying God within that person. It is our job to receive and to be grateful.

Jen: *That's why I think some of our greatest teachers in receiving are toddlers, babies, children.*

Janelle: Yes, because they're like, "Give it more."

Jen: *They'll go out and pick a weed. They see beauty in the weed. They don't have anything to give to you but their love and the little gems that they might find outdoors. So it's all their heart going in and saying, "I found you this beautiful flower." It's special. It's teaching that here it is. I probably speak for most of us. We all melt when we get this from little kids because they just got that feeling, and it opens you up.*

Janelle: Right. It doesn't matter whether you're going to use it or not or whether you think it's beneficial or not. It's just the act of saying yes to.

Jen: *Right, because if you're closed off, and I guess as you said, there's an ebb and flow, so all of us at one point or another are open and closed. If you're closed off on an individual or small group level, are you always closing yourself off then from the universe in terms of receiving or is the universe always going to find a way in?*

Janelle: It's eventually going to be to where you have no choice but to accept that you're a Divine Plan. I mean, it's just either you're going to learn through your pain or you're going to learn through joy. Either you're going to get hit over the head or you're going to willingly go in, one of the two.

Either of which is going to happen and you're going to have to get on the train no matter what. You can get there through religion. You can get there through spirituality. It doesn't matter, but eventually you have to succumb to that there's an undeniable force in your life and being generous with that energy is part of our gift in each other, is to be able to take in energy and then whether it's through an item or whatever, and give it to someone else.

Jen: *Okay. Again, do you feel like this is the time where if people remember to connect and ask for help in everything they do, that as a whole, we can all kind of get it more easily than we would 10 years ago, 20 years ago?*

Janelle: Absolutely, because the energy is moving quicker. It's faster. Things are showing up quickly. Hesitation is our biggest hurdle. We think we have to know the ins and outs of everything before we take the step. Sometimes we have to jump quickly before we miss the opportunity.

Jen: *One more thing before we move to a break: is this something your Team is constantly saying, "Hey, Janelle, you got to teach people how to be better at receiving?" because it opens up the gateway, because once we all learn how to receive, as you said, our journey and what we're here to do is going to get that much easier, right, and we're just going to have those connections. The connections that we need will be made that much easier, and we'll enlighten our way as we move.*

Janelle: Yes, it is something that I didn't understand that I was doing so well until I started asking the question. Why does it occur as not easier for me, but because it's not always easier, but it is something I rely on. I think that's the difference in what I was doing differently and most spiritual people I have run across. They do rely on it. I rely on that. I don't want to do it alone. It's something that I understood I was doing differently, that I needed to help educate and help us understand that as people, one of our greatest gifts is how well we can spread the abundance.

Jen: *Janelle, I just want to read to you something you posted on Facebook today, and then talk a little bit more about receiving. You said, "If you are open to it, the whole universe will move through you fully and move you to be all you can be. The trick is to be open enough to let it come through and how many moments in a day do you block the universe?"*

I feel like you are telling our listeners exactly how to unblock today by feeling worthy, and asking for help in all the little things that we do. I'm going to just sort of throw that at you to expand a little bit on it and tell us.

Janelle: Yes, that's totally exactly what they say to me at any given moment, "Please ask for assistance. We're waiting for you. Please ask us to help," because we are meant to support each other, both physically not just from the universe, but to say to you, Jen, "Hey, can you help me with this because I don't understand it. Do you know how to work out this?" or you know, to be vulnerable enough to ask physical people to help us.

When they show up with asking a question, "I need help with this," we're open to little kids, like you said, giving us a flower or something like that, but when it comes to an adult who is offering assistance, we often have the thought of, "Well, what am I going to have to give you in order to accept this gift?"

Jen: *Right, yes, absolutely. Yes, I think many people may struggle with an undercurrent of, if you do this for me, then what am I'm going to have to do for you?*

Janelle: I'm going to have to owe you something instead of just understanding that that was just a gift and meant from a place of receiving or giving you abundance.

I can't tell you how many times I've been somewhere, let's say, and I'll run and go buy somebody's dinner without them knowing that I'm doing it. The waiter will say to me, "Well, why are you doing that? You don't know them."

"Yes, absolutely, that's exactly why I'm doing it." He goes, "Do you want me to put your name on it?" "No, I don't."

Jen: *However, when I receive gifts from children, and again, they're just giving something to me and I think because I'm so open, it always feels so good. But I clearly understand the feeling of perhaps the universe moving through them. With adults, that feeling is not always there. I guess it must be from this feeling of obligation or strings attached.*

Janelle: It totally is. Just remember that that is still that same child that the universe is moving through to bring you whatever you asked for, and it may be this is the other thing, too. We think we know what we need.

Jen: *Right, we don't have any idea.*

Janelle: We really don't. Yes, we really think, "I know exactly what I need." I can't tell you how many times myself I've asked for assistance with something and said specifically, "I need this," and they send me something that's not even related to what I asked for.

I go, "How is that related?" I just ask the question but I expect whatever is coming through because I know maybe I don't know what I need.

Jen: *Okay. Again, I want to remind the listeners what you said earlier, Janelle, in terms of receiving that the universe is going to use any and all means to get to us.*

When you're asking, what's going to come back is either through a person or a song, or some kind of sign to you. The trick is to be open to it and to hopefully recognize it when it comes back in.

Janelle, how often do you see this in children? You know, as children move through the school system, I think there's a big— for lack of a better word— wrestling with receiving. I think it changes or can change for them depending on how you help kids because they're the next generation coming up.

They're the ones. Obviously they're our teachers. How do we keep them open to this? If we start to see them veer off from being so open to suddenly being a little bit closed year by year?

Janelle: Right. For me and my house, it's a daily conversation. My kids see me literally say out loud, "Hey, Team, I need some help." I don't care who is listening to me. I don't care who is around. I don't care.

That's because I don't have the embarrassment factor but as my teenager looks at me and she's like, "Oh my gosh, mom," I catch her asking. I catch her asking though. If she's preparing for a test in school, in the morning, I say, "Okay, make sure you ask your angels for help, make sure you ask your teachers on the other side for assistance in helping remember what it is that you learn and staying focused," and she does it.

I think I know that I'm not, as far as spiritual parenting, I know I'm not the only one who probably teaches their children to ask for assistance, but I think it's a slim majority of us that do. I think it does need to be through demonstration.

They need to see us as parents being open to asking for help because we're trained as parents to act like we have all the answers and we know exactly what to do next, and we've got it all figured out. The truth is, as I will say to them, I don't know.

Jen: *Right, you do actually always seem to say, "I don't know, let's ask. The universe will use every means possible to give us an answer."*

Can you help us understand how we can all be sure that we've gotten the answer? Do people feel it in a feeling? Do they just recognize it? How do we recognize that communication?

We talked a little bit about the means that the universe is going to use, but in your experience, what do you tell clients that ask you the same question? How do they know it's the message for them? How do they understand that they've gotten it?

Janelle: Right, the piece that I would say above anything else is that there's a current to it. When I say current, it's a feeling but it feels like peace, neutral. It's not negative or positive. It feels neutral.

A lot of people mistake messages as these big neon light moments, like you're going to be walking down the street, and somebody is going to put a big poster board in front of your face that says, "Turn left." No, pretty much you can guarantee that's not going to happen. They are very subtle, subtle moments. At times in my own experience, as connected as I am, if I know, if I were to blink in that moment, I would have missed what they were trying to show me. I say they're little bitty wisps of hair in the air that you really have to slow down, breathe, and look at what's being presented to you because the truth is, we really miss no less than 100 messages a day.

Jen: *Wow. All right, again, we've got about a minute or so before we break for another song. How many messages a day, if you could throw a number out there, do you think we all get? If we're missing 100, are we getting 2000, 10,000?*

Janelle: Oh, it's exponential, enormous, because you've got to remember we're vibrational beings. We're sending out a current all the time. As every living plant, every other person that we come in contact with, every ancestor, every loved one that's crossed over, every angel, all of that is sending currents into the universe, okay, that's a lot.

Plus, you got the Internet, and then you've got cell phones. Then you've got everything else. It's no wonder that we may miss most of them and get the one that we needed to get.

The thing is that the one that comes through is going to be a brush on the cheek. That's how soft it is. It will have the feeling of neutral, means that it makes you feel at peace, at ease within yourself. That's how you know it's a message for you.

Keith: *With that, we're going to take our last break. I guess nobody really wants to call in today because Janelle and Jen have just hit the sweet spot. Everybody just wants to listen rather than ask questions about themselves. That's really good.*

Jen: *Okay, welcome back. This is Spiritual Happy Hour with Jennifer Louziotis and Janelle Hoyland. Spiritual Happy Hour is a show that helps you learn to live with your spiritual self, lead your life with your spiritual self first.*

Today, we are having an entire discussion on receiving and feeling loved and worthy. This is the first time that we've done our show where we actually haven't gotten any phone calls. Janelle was pointing out to Keith and I, this is directly related to receiving because many shows, all the shows we've done before, we've always gotten calls.

People have always wanted help but as Keith pointed out to me in the break, isn't it interesting that when we are actually talking about receiving, nobody is calling? So I'm going to turn it over to you, Janelle, and have you give us your thoughts on this.

Janelle: Absolutely, it's directly related. In the sense of when you say, "Okay, we're going to throw down the gauntlet and say how do we get there ourselves? How do we ask for assistance and step into abundance, and allowing the universe to support us in all that we are?" Okay, we're doing the show on that, and the energy is connected to that, and connected to supporting you, giving you direct guidance about how to open, your field up so that you know without a doubt that whatever you ask for will show up.

Maybe not in the way you want it to be, or in the way that you think it should show up for you, but in the way the universe says, this is the most appropriate way for it to show up for you.

Jen: *Right, that's been a gift.*

Janelle: Exactly. The very fact that out of all the shows that we have, there's no callers means exactly that. This is a demonstration of where we're at in worthiness, in accepting assistance.

The thing is we really want it. We really hunger for it, but we're so blocked and unready to receive.

Jen: *We're just wrapped up in feeling unworthy or unloved or afraid.*
Janelle: Yes, totally. You know what, it makes us uncomfortable.

Jen: *Yes, you can feel it.*

Janelle: The topic of receiving makes us uncomfortable.

Jen: *It's funny because I'm not uncomfortable. Keith and I, and you, we're all hanging out, but it's like I said to him, it's like that Bugs Bunny cartoon with the singing frog that only sang for the owner. Once the frog was on stage he wouldn't sing. Everyone was looking at him and he was like, "Ribbit."*

Again, I hope that people will tune into this show in the archives so that we get this message out. Ask for help. Know that it will be there for you to guide you, and really, I guess Janelle, it's like the first baby step, isn't it, because if you can't ask for help and be open, how are you going to walk through that journey?

Janelle: Exactly. You want to always search for it outside of you. You're always going to look for someone else to fix it. Let me go to the next guru or the next reader, healer, mentor, whatever, the next self-help book, instead of going within and saying, "You know what, all of my resources are available to me. How do I move into that frequency of allowing myself to receive everything that I've ever asked for?"

The truth is, it's not unavailable to you. Every dream that you've ever thought about, every desire that you've ever had is available to you. It's how quickly can you move into that alignment.

Jen: *Again, to recap what you said the last segment, "It's a feeling of peace that will hold weight over you or that you'll have, a neutral but yet peaceful feeling when you make that connection of that help is there for you."*

*Again, you said—I love what you said on Facebook last week: "If you are open to it, the whole universe,"—**the whole universe**— "will move through you so you fully move through, so you can be all you can be."*

Janelle: Exactly.

Jen: *As you said last week, this is the time. This is a fantastic time to be alive. We're all making the shift, so let's all feel worthy enough to ask those questions. If all we have to do is ask, really, we can all do that. We just have to remember.*

Janelle: It's an uncomfortable place. We feel like it makes us weak, it makes us unknowledgeable, whatever the case may be. I'm quick to tell you if I don't know, I'm going to ask. I'm not at all shy about that. You'll hear me say in session, "Let me ask. I don't know. Let me see. I don't know."

Jen: *That is true, you say that all the time, "I don't know. Hold on, let me ask," then you go, "Hold on, hold on," and you wait a minute, and there it is. You get that clear peaceful feeling that you know the message comes back through. Then you go from there.*

Janelle: Exactly. This will be one of those ones that's in the archives. You know what? We're pushing a gauntlet of something that is a current on the planet that I think is beyond our time a little bit. We're ahead of the game.

Jen: *Got it. That is a perfect way to wrap up this show. Thanks again for tuning in and we'll see you guys soon.*

Show 5 – Receiving
Numerology perspective by Jen
Life Path number 4

I find it interesting that the Receiving show is connected to the energy of 4 which is associated with hard work, determination and putting things in order or in place. We learn how to open ourselves up to receive anything we can dream about during this show. For me, I think the Universe was trying to show us where we are in our thinking about receiving, in that we think it is hard work. It doesn't have to be hard work at all and that's what I think they showed us in the end. We need to remember that life is supposed to be fun.

Show 6 – Procrastination
Air Date: July 25, 2013
Life Path number 11

Jen: *So do you want to talk a little bit about procrastination? What is procrastination and what does it mean from a spiritual sense?*

Janelle: Even for my procrastination, even for myself, I feel like, you know, I at some places, I stop myself from doing what it is that I'm called to do, even for me. I don't feel like I keep up enough that kind of thing. And that's all the ego. Spirit always brings no more or no less than we can do. And often I find—most of the time, we feel we're not capable of doing what we are called to do, and so we put blocks in our way, such as having too many to-do lists, you know or the health stuff, or work stuff, you know. There's not enough time; I'm too tired, whatever the case may be. We definitely set ourselves up for not succeeding because we're afraid of being powerful.

Jen: *Does everybody do this, and how often does everybody do this? Do people do this like five times a day, or...*

Janelle: OH! Oh my goodness. Yeah, it's an epidemic...

We-we, you know, it's one of the things that I see that we struggle with most, is we like to say, "I'll get to it," or "I don't have enough time." "There's other things to do" And the other part of it is that if we actually cross off what's on this spiritual to-do list, we might actually be happy. Scary. We might actually not have anything to complain about, hmmm.

Jen: *Do all of us unconsciously know we have a spiritual to-do list? You know, because we all flood ourselves with, "Oh I've got to clean the house; I've got to clean my room; I've got to do the laundry; I've got to do this; I've got to do that." So do we all know our spiritual to-do list, and if we don't, how do we get in touch with what we think our big to-do list is and what we are here to do?*

Janelle: We all have it. It's all in your DNA. It is the nudge or the beckoning that you hear, the little tick of the clock within you that says that there's something more; that there's something greater. And it's not always like this big life-changing thing, you know. Sometimes it's just about, you know, showing up at work and being 100% you and being joyous; or being unapologetic for living your fullest expression wherever you are. And we're always aware of it; we're always aware of it. Your spirit knows. Your cognitive mind, not your ego mind, your logistical mind, may not want to surrender to that.

Jen: *I was going to say; so how do you get yourself to stop procrastinating? How do you stop taking the long way to work, or how do you stop, you know, doing the laundry instead of sitting down to do what you need to do? And how do you also know when you do need to do the laundry? How do we learn to strike a balance?*

Janelle: The biggest clue that I see is how much agitation you have within you. How much frustration do you have within you? How much unsettled energy do you feel inside you? That's how much you know that you're procrastinating. In anything, it can be procrastinating in cleaning house; it could be procrastinating in doing your spiritual path. But it's the level of discomfort that you feel in your being: you feel unsettled. And the surest way that I know how to get out of it is to get quiet for a second; go for a walk, you know, or you know, do something that disconnects your mind; that you can actually "feel" what it is that you need to do. The feeling is what I follow.

Jen: *Okay, so you know what your first step is.*

Janelle: Yes.

Jen: *Okay. Again, I want to go back to though, your spiritual to-do list versus the other to-do list. And again, being in alignment or understanding how you know if you're even ticking off things on your spiritual to-do list. Because it's so fascinating to me, because you've never used that before. And I kind of like that "spiritual to-do list."*

Janelle: Well, you know, with me, I always bring in the right alignment.

Jen: *Yeah, exactly, so you go out there and grab the to-do list. And we've had to put spiritual in front of it.*

Janelle: I, you know, the, the, the calling or the spiritual to-do list, or the purpose list, right? It's all of the things that are your higher program here. You know, they're not the doing the dishes, they're not, it's whatever your soul came in to let people experience through you. So that could be writing a book; that could be singing a great song; that could be, you know, dancing; it could be, you know, doing the radio show; you know, whatever, whatever's on that to-do list is what the Universe, or God, or the Light is calling you to do is greater than you can imagine for yourself. So even the idea, right? ...is limited based on what they want you to do, or what they're asking of you. And so what occurs is that we feel too small; we feel inadequate; and that's the ego self; that's the human self that likes to keep us in the lower frequencies and doesn't allow us to step into and that's why procrastination comes up because it doesn't allow us to step into that alternate reality that we don't know ourselves in. And the truth is, we like being comfortable, so even procrastination it causes discomfort in your being. It's still a comfortable place; it's an excuse; it's a tolerance. And we get comfortable with that because we like to say, "Oh you know, I'll get to it." We like to have something just-just out of sorts.

Jen: *Well, I think it can become habit, too—because this is how I used to write papers in school. I had to clean my apartment first. So in grad school I would say to myself, "Oh, I have to sit down and clean; I need to have an hour of cleaning and then I can sit down because things will be peaceful around me." And I never, I never got rid of that habit. I always, even today, I must clean; I have to go clean first before I do whatever. So what, what would happen if you just did whatever first?*

Janelle That you give yourself permission to do what your spirit is calling you to do; it would free up the energy around you in order to bring you something that you didn't see coming.

Jen: *OOOH! Oh my gosh! So it's like even, even more of a-a surprise at the end, almost like your Happy Meal with a surprise inside. So in other words, by procrastinating and throwing yourself, or keeping yourself in that limited energy, you lose out on exponential gifts that you don't even know might even be there just by sitting down to do it. Is that right?*

Janelle: Yes. And the truth, it's like saying "yes" to yourself.

Jen: *Is it saying yes to your intuition? The more you say yes to your intuition, the stronger it gets; the more you put yourself first and say yes to yourself; the more you're going to get whatever you need for you and for everybody else.*

Janelle: Yes...

Jen: *Turn around; heal yourself; heal the world.*

Janelle: Yes. Because you ARE the biggest demonstration. It doesn't matter what you feel the calling, the purpose is. It's just how much are you willing to say yes to you?

Jen: *See, it's so interesting when you put it that way; it's just you saying yes to you. I always forget to turn the mirror back to myself. Janelle, you've run into this before and you and I talk about this all the time. Why is this so hard? If we all chose to come to planet earth, right? And we all have come from greatness anyway, why do we all struggle with this so much? Why is it so common?*

Janelle: Because we...we...we...we are conditioned by the world around us; by other people seeing us; by the witness that we are in the world; to live in a limited reality. And the truth is, that if we were to step out and to live in the fullness of who you are; saying yes to yourself all the time; there is infinite abundance in every single area. There's not limited supply in anything.

Jen: *Right... because we say this all the time on the show; that there's unlimited supply in everything. But you never phrased it as such, as just as it's as easy as saying yes to yourself. Right? It's* *not necessarily about what you have to do, such as "I've got to go to work; I've got to do this, I've got to do that." It's saying yes to who you are.*

Janelle: [talking over] Yeah!

Jen: *I always ask about topics from the perspective of a child, because, you know, I have kids and I'm just also curious to know about the next generation coming in. Do they struggle with this? Or are they just learning from us? So if I'm a procrastinator are my kids going to do that, or is this next line of children coming in not having to necessarily deal with this as much? Are we going to break the barrier for them, or is this going to be something that they're going to struggle with or potentially struggle with as well?*

Janelle: Well, it's interesting. I have a 16-year old, and then I have this two-year old. You know? In the sixteen-year old, I see it more than I do in my two-year old. And not because of the age; but because of their spiritual connection. So I, I'm understanding that the, the younger generations are more connected than say, my sixteen-year old. Um, and so, whereas they'll still look at the world to define them; the two-year old doesn't look at the world to define him.

We look at the world to define us instead of looking within to define us.

Jen: *Right... That's why I like your catch phrase, "Say yes to you." That makes total sense to me. It's like "Say yes to yourself" helps you remember that this lifetime is about you; this is about you and your gifts that you came in to share with everybody in your own unique way that again, you always say connects everybody to one another.*

But how to do you stop? I always feel like I want to put the brakes on kids before they hit school; or before they become of age where they start to want to not pay attention, but they want other people to like them more so they stop, you know, remembering that they just have to say yes to them. Do you know what I mean? How do we put the brakes on that? How do you provide the example?

Janelle: Right, well, that, so always live in the reality of—uh, we want to change the world. There's always something within us that says, "I want to change the world; I want to change my experience," right? And like with my sixteen-year old, she is watching me demonstrate in my life how much I say yes to myself, or how much I limit myself and my expression.

Jen: *Okay.*

Janelle: Gauging. She's watching me gauge that experience. And all of my kids are mainstream kids; which means they're in regular schools; public schools; they're around other kids, but I give them, I give them full permission to go after what it is that their soul is calling them to do. No matter what. And so when they live in that reality at home, then okay, you can imagine what that's doing in their world, right?

Jen: *Right...right.*

Janelle: They have the witness around them of, and it comes up, it comes up, it has come up with them. Like my sixteen-year old last year in school, she had a girl who was, you know, aggressive towards her, you know, with things, with things about her at school—da, da, da da—and she looked at me and said, "Mom, that's not about me; it's not about me; she's insecure; there is a fear within her."

Jen: *Right. Good for her! Right.*

Janelle: She's sixteen! That's not a normal sixteen-year-old conversation. But because of my conversations with her...

Jen: *Right. But it's amazing that something...when you take something that doesn't feel at all for me, connected to this bigger issue with you and your daughter, right? If you had said to me yesterday, "Okay, procrastination." I would never have connected the dots to how procrastination means NOT saying yes to yourself. When you say yes to yourself and you bear witness to yourself, you provide the example and it trickles down to everyone around you. And so therefore procrastination is even related to parenting...which I would sort of get it, but not get it until you put it in that perspective. I think that was just so powerful.*

Janelle: The other thing that was coming up in our conversation too...uh between you and I, Jen is that we, we, we sometimes get confused with our purpose and earning a living.

Jen: *Absolutely.*

Janelle: And having abundance, and in that way, and so we-we limit ourselves in our expression that way. That's another way of us saying, "Well, you know, if I'm not really working hard at my purpose here, I'm not working AS my purpose," then I can use that as an excuse for not living full out.

Jen: *I think people really do struggle with what you and I were saying (in regards to work). They may say, "Okay, I need to get out there and work my purpose;" but then, but if you're going to share yourself as a whole doing anything in life; then that's still a gift to others, right? So even if you're not living your purpose, you're still a gift. You're just being somewhere working is still a gift to others.*

So even if you're not working your purpose, you're still sharing yourself and it's still what you're here to do.

Janelle: Right. Exactly. It's not the, it's not everyone, you know, Changing the world is changing it where you are. Being the demonstration where you are, and sometimes yeah, some people are meant to earn a living doing what they're called to do. But sometimes when the abundance is, is kind of dormant and that...it means that you need to say yes to something else in order to learn something about yourself. So that might be, going and getting a part-time job in addition to doing what your work is on the side.

Jen: *Well, because you free up, you don't have fear going through.*

Janelle: You free up the energy.

Jen: *And I, I do see that's common. I think this comes up a lot for people, too, in terms of blocking and how to know where you fit in or where you allow yourself to fit in. And that it's okay to not be doing something that has a huge purpose.*

Janelle: Spiritual. (spiritual purpose)

Jen: *Janelle, do you just want to do a little wrap up with me then, today on procrastination, what we should all take away. What's the take-away, I guess?*

Janelle: Well, I think when I ask the question, "What else does spirit or the universe, or angels bring to the table"? And they said, one of the things that is the most important is to realize that procrastination is like what we were talking about before, it's not a uh, block in the sense of denying yourself, but it's more about all the context that we like to live in order to prevent us to from getting where we need to be. And it's another one of those ego trips; you know that likes to, uh stand in your way. And one of the things that often comes up for me, is that I do live in that there's infinite time to get everything done. And it's a weird thing that I know not a lot of people live in; but times on my side, you know? So Jen, you know that from demonstration; but I like to work with time. Time is my friend. So we have a great conversation; and time serves me well. So I have all the time I need to get everything done in the sense of, "Okay, I've got this done." and I don't have guilt around the things that I don't get done. I don't have any guilt related to that. And I know, that's, you know, a rare commodity to find; but I don't. I don't have guilt in how well my kids are doing; I'm good with that.

Jen: *So do you just, in terms of not getting it all done; do you just put it on tomorrow's burner? Do you say "Oh, all right, got this done; didn't get that done, I'll just do that tomorrow"? Or "It wasn't for me to do"?*

Janelle: Well, the thing is, do you want to, if you ask your spirit, "Do you really want to cross everything off your list?"

Jen: *Right...then your spirit will say, "No. No! I'd rather do this or that?" So then you know it's important. I guess it floats to the top, all right. And with your kids.*

Janelle: ...and in a spiritual sense...yeah.

Jen: *And so then with your kids, do you just know that it's their own process? And so you're fine with what's going to happen for them is going to happen for them? I'm throwing it out there because I think so many of us have guilt about you know, what our kids did or didn't do or what we can provide for them or don't, or are not able to provide for them, etcetera and so on.*

Janelle: Yeah, I mean, if I, I look—here's the thing. You know, there are things that have come up with my kids, you know, that they've had to go through and learn through or walk through with me and it's you know, when those moments of guilt come up, I just admit them and say, "Okay, I'm feeling guilty about this" Um...yeah. I probably should have made a different decision. That's fine. I don't hold those vibrations. And I also hold the highest intention for them, to live a full expression here. So whenever I look at them; whenever I have a conversation with them; it's always in the highest light. So I hold the vision; not my choices for them; but what are their choices for them, in order for them to live to their highest—highest expression here.

Jen: *I also like what you said, too; you don't hold the guilt; you don't hold onto it; you experience it and let it go.*

Janelle: Let it go. And that's the energy of connecting with the Holy Spirit, if you would; or light energy is to allow those emotions to come up and let them be free with you to not hold them. The more that we block ourselves and hold it back, it's another way of keeping us from ourselves.

Jen: *And today you also kept bringing up the current, like letting people flow in a current. And I think that that's really true to remember that things have to flow.*

Janelle: They have to!

Jen: *Right...okay...it's the opposite of procrastination. Let it flow.*

Janelle: Yes, so give yourself, the basic thing is to give yourself permission to procrastinate; therefore, you're not making it right or wrong.

Jen: *Got it, okay, all right. Well that's pretty powerful.*

Show 6 – Procrastination
Numerology perspective by Jen
Life Path number 11

I felt like I was going in circles before we broadcast this show. I let fear take over and put the show on the back burner so it is interesting that they brought in the energy of the 11 as part of the procrastination show. In this show we talk about having a Spiritual To Do list that is connected to your purpose on Earth and is encoded in your DNA. The underlying energy of the 11 serves to reflect and strengthen that point with the traits of intuition, connection to the subconscious, being a visionary, and combined with the number 2 are that of peacemaker, harmony and balance in relationships. We were reminded of our partnership with the Universe in this show and of our own ability to follow our intuition as we co-create the life of our dreams.

The second section added together—shows 4 to 6
Life Path number 3

When I added the Life Path numbers of shows 3 through 5 together and reduced the sum to a single digit I got the number 3. Life Path Number 3 is associated with creativity, self-expression and sharing your story through creative works. We are all here to share our own individual talents and gifts with the world and this section shows us how to get back in touch with what our soul is meant to share and be in this life time and the energy of the 3 can help us share that with others collectively.

CHAPTER THREE
SHOT OF TEQUILA
"INTENTION"

Show 7 – Intention Part 1: Manifesting: Creating your destiny
Show 8 – Intention Part 2: Facing Fears
Show 9 – Intention Part 3: Taking Action

We didn't set out to create a three-part series on Intentions but it turned out that the Universe had a lot of information to give to us and it couldn't be relayed in one show. However, our guides didn't share that information with us during our weekly planning call. This was a real turning point for me in terms of allowing myself to be led by the Universe and to trust that they knew what the listeners needed to hear more than we did. The weekly calls were also part of my learning process for relying on my own intuition. I got to practice asking a question, tuning into my intuition for an answer and sharing that information with Janelle as confirmation that what I received really was Divine guidance. In terms of this series of shows, I had to ask if all the information was relayed to the listeners after each show and if I felt that the listeners "got it," or if the message was complete. I literally had to ask the question in my mind and then check in and feel for an answer in my body and then check in with Janelle. After the first and second shows, it didn't feel complete to me or Janelle so we ended up adding another two shows on intention.

When we both decided that we wanted to broadcast a show about setting intentions, Janelle paused during our first planning call and said "hold on." I knew she was receiving guidance, but I could also feel the energy around me shift. I could feel the air in my house move. Janelle came back on the phone and I asked her to explain what had just occurred. She said the Universe just shifted the space, energy and vibration around our show for everyone. She continued to explain to me that setting an intention is usually done during the months of December and January, not October, so our vibration and the vibration of the show had to be lifted for us to better receive the information. As I understood it, I think they had to bring the vibration and energy of the future (December/January) into the present time (October) and at the same time they moved our energy or vibration forward.

I was fascinated by this shift of energy, but I didn't understand that this act was an example of the Universe supporting our intention for the show right in front of me. I didn't get the depth of what was occurring. It was a demonstration of what can occur in your life if you give one hundred percent faith and trust in the Universe and follow your Divine plan. We were co-creating here. We were in the process of jointly setting an intention and the Universe was showing us an example of not only how they were supporting that intention but *contributing* to it by shifting space.

I knew it wasn't just me and Janelle going on air week after week. I knew our guides were present and that God/Universe was present, but at the same time I still missed a ton of signs (in this case a HUGE sign, or example) of how the Universe is working in our favor, one hundred percent of the time and for our highest good. I understood that space shifted because I could feel it shift, but missed that it was a direct example of what we were going to talk about.

I may have missed this demonstration because I was so focused on my marriage during the time we broadcast these next three shows. I had set an intention with my husband around his newly formed business and my attention was focused on the outcome of our intention. I wasn't paying attention to many details of life at that time. I was in waiting mode. Waiting for the Universe to bring what I wanted for me and Dee, the both of us. That wanting, waiting and worrying was actually blocking our intention altogether.

I love my husband with all my heart. He really is my best friend. He has always supported me in everything I do. Words can't express my love for him. At the time we were broadcasting the shows on intention, my husband had recently decided to start his own company with a group of colleagues. This was something he had dreamed about since the time I'd met him. Every now and then he would mention this dream to me and I could feel how much owning his own company meant to him. He always said if the opportunity presented itself, it wasn't going to be a quick decision. He would have to meet the right set of people to work with and timing for the family would have to be in alignment before he would take this type of risk. Shortly after we returned from Japan, an opportunity presented itself. We talked about it and I said I fully supported him in his dream of owning his own company (or so I thought at the time). So he set out with a group of colleagues and they got to work creating their new business.

In truth, I wasn't being completely honest with myself or my husband when it came to his new company. On the one hand, I did support his dream and I wanted him to go after it, but I was afraid of the financial risk we were taking as well and the energy of that fear seeped in to our intention and really affected the energy of our household and I'm sure my husband's energy overall.

I learned from Janelle that when we set an intention, we hold the vibration for it to manifest, but we can also hold fears underneath that intention that actually block it from getting to us or being created. Or we can actually set an intention, but set it from a place of unworthiness, and doing that also negates the intention because we are asking for something we don't feel worthy of having and we need to actually match on an energy level what it is we are trying to bring into our lives.

You can't bring in what you don't feel worthy of having. What we send out is what we get back to us. I knew this to be true and had read this before in many books on spirituality, but I never knew or felt how the *depth* of my thoughts and fears could block what we were trying to bring in to our life. Types of fears that can hold us back include fear of not enough money, not enough time, fear of failure, or some outside source like a family member can hold a fear and this can make the other person diminish their light because they unconsciously can feel the other person's discomfort.

That's what was happening in my family. Dee was going after the opportunity of a lifetime and so was I in broadcasting the show. However, he was steamrolling ahead without fear and I was slogging along making slow progress. A fear of abandonment and my own worthiness issues were coming up for me, but instead of accepting those, looking at the lesson that was coming up for me and releasing those fears, I focused on the fact that we were no longer getting a regular pay check, and the lack of financial stability was very disconcerting for me. In reality, we had planned for this new job and there wasn't any instability occurring at all.

There may not have been a physical paycheck coming in each month, but there was stability.

Deep down what I really feared was how Dee's success would affect our relationship. If Dee got really successful and I didn't, what would he think of me? Would he still love me in the same way? What did I have to show for myself? Was it "good enough" to match his success? Furthermore, I held on to this belief that success in business meant something had to be sacrificed and for me that meant family time. So, I feared the more successful he became, the less time he would have to spend with us. I didn't focus on the abandonment as much as I focused on the lack of a regular paycheck. For some reason, I blew that way out of proportion and I would become stressed about money toward the end of every month.

I have no doubt the energy of my fears affected my husband on multiple levels at home and at work. In fact, I used to watch this type of scenario play out in Tokyo during the four years we lived there. Whenever we would meet a family that was new to Japan, there was a surefire way to tell if they would "make it" or last the duration of their contract in Asia. If one partner wanted to come to Asia and the other one didn't but said yes anyway, there was an energy of instability that showed in the partnership from the time they set foot in Japan. Oftentimes, the working spouse of those couples would not do well at work because they were spending energy trying to support the other partner. They were diminishing their light or holding back to support the other partner, but they were hurting the whole in the process.

When Dee and I decided to move to Japan, we were both one hundred percent equally invested in our decision to go. I didn't have any underlying fears during that time and we had great success together. With his new company, I held on to fear and he did diminish his light, unconsciously, because he could feel my doubt. I needed once more to look at my fears for what they were, talk about them and release them. Many times Dee would come to me and say, "How can I make you more comfortable with my working on my own?" The answer had nothing to do with Dee. I had to step into my own power and turn my efforts back to the show. I just needed to trust him one hundred percent like I did in Japan. By trusting him, I would be trusting the overall plan the Universe had for each of us.

We did have this very conversation one night and I made a choice to put one hundred percent faith in him and the company. What I did differently that night was to check in with my intuition and I actually surrendered all my fears surrounding the company. Within two days of my surrendering and resetting our intention together we received ten checks of unclaimed funds that were in our name. All ten checks totaled over thirteen thousand dollars. I think this was a sign from the Universe brought to me by way of a paycheck. The Universe was saying they had our back and they chose checks to show me no matter what I am afraid of, we always have full support.

Show 7 – Intention Part 1: Manifest Your Destiny

Air Date: November 11, 2013

Life Path number 1

Jen: *Hi, everybody. It's Jen, Janelle and Keith and we think Keith has finally solved our sound issue, I hope. Janelle, can you hear us?*

Janelle: I can hear you.

Jen: *Great. So we are not using a regular microphone at all. That has been going on for the last half hour. Keith and I have been trouble-shooting. My biggest fear is doing this show and making a fool out of myself with technical issues and I guess I faced that fear today.*

I can't tell you how many people were texting me saying, "I can hear you on mine. I can hear you." I thanked them because you need to know what you're broadcasting. So thank you to all the listeners saying that.

And I kept texting back, "We know, we're trying to fix this. We're trying to fix it." Right, Keith?

Janelle, should we just jump ahead? Or do you want to say anything about the technical issues from your end before we get to the topic? I don't care either way. This is kind of like a no holds barred show.

Janelle: What's so funny for me is that from here I can see all of the conundrum of issues that you're having and then Keith having these light bulbs go off like, "I think it's this." And doing all this stuff.

When you finally got to where we were just about to hear each other, the feedback was sounding like an alien from another planet. It was quite funny on my end. It was like squealing and alien noises coming through. Which is great. That's a fun experience.

Jen: *Janelle, when you and I try to figure out topics for the show, we talk sometimes right before the show, sometimes we talk two or three days before the show. And this time we talked a couple days ago about creating your destiny and your intention.*

We were on the phone and I'll just give it from my perspective. Janelle, as she sometimes does when I'm on the phone with her, stops to check in with her guides. And this time she stopped for quite a while.

And when she came back up to connect with me, I said to her, "You just changed the space for the show. What happened?" So Janelle, if you want to tell the listeners, because I think this is a really special show despite all the technical difficulties that we had getting on air.

I'm really excited for this show. So if you just want to explain what you had to do for all of us to get us all ready for the show on that level.

Janelle: Right. Well normally you think of intentions as something that you do at the beginning of the year. Your resolutions or the things that you want to create for the New Year.

And so what was occurring for me, and this is why I kind of heard my Team interrupt us, was that they shifted the energy so that it could come through now and help manifest things for the New Year. And the space was that it needed to happen or occur that day. And also, too, with all of the technical issues we were having, it's because it's such a high vibration of energy that came in. Not only in our conversation as far as shifting things and bringing things to our consciousness or awareness, but moving them into this plane. It messes with all kinds of electrical equipment. It's just a fact. So that was part of the issue. That's why on my end I was trying to make a bartering system. "Can we work on this a little bit? We've got to get this here."

So normally it would be something that I would do in the beginning of the year. But it was so needed by everyone else that they made a special, let's say, energy or a movement to create it to happen here today.

Jen: *Which I just think is amazing because I say this all the time on the show, but we are all energy. And I have to tell you, when I was on the phone with Janelle planning this show, I knew exactly what was going on. I said to her, "Holy cow, you're shifting the space."*

So again, with all the technical difficulties, my mind is like I've gone on empty, which is very rare for me because normally I think too much. I'm going to throw it over to you, Janelle and ask you how you would like to start talking about creating your destiny?

Because with all this shifting, I'm a blank slate.

Janelle: Your brain shut off a little bit. That's good. I actually like that. There's a couple of things that come up. We'll look at three of the issues that happen when we're trying to create something to occur in our life.

So here's the thing: we always hear when you're manifesting intentions or you're thinking about intentions that you hold the thought for them. You concentrate. You have the message written down somewhere. Affirmations or what have you. But what we don't realize is we can be our own stopping place. And it's not that in my own life that I don't experience constricted energy or something takes a little bit longer to create. It happens with me all the time. It's just that I'm used to just barreling through. Unless it's something that I need to look at. Which sometimes happens if I have a fear that's coming up or I have a block that I need to look at.

So this is what occurs: You have the idea pop into your mind. (For example) I'd love to let's say go on a trip. Just one example. So you have this wonderful possibility of something that really makes your heart sing and really cultivates passion within you. So you hold that vibration. Then you think about it for a minute.

I don't have the money, one. I don't have the time. So we come up with all of these reasons that it's not possible. This is the first thing that we do.

The second thing we do is we don't realize that we're also sending out another vibration underneath that. If you don't come up with any reasons why, there's usually the fear of failure; that I'm going to get there and something is going to stop me. I'm going to get sick or something is going to happen with the plane or someone in my family is going to need me. Whatever the case may be.

So we put in other roadblocks that may be subconscious that are running another program underneath what we're doing. The other part of it that comes into this is the third thing.

We set intentions based on our highest soul's desire. But let's say through religion, through our family's experience, stepping into that place may also be pushing other people's boundaries. So then we don't try, because we don't want to be excluded from how our family sees us. We see that as a negative.

Jen: *So we subconsciously or sometimes consciously feel them either pulling away or reacting to this intention, whether it's spoken or unspoken?*

Janelle: Right. They can feel you changing and going after something. And let's say they may not be living a life of their highest intentions. They may not be loving themselves fully. They may not be saying yes to the things that would make them happy. So the case is that when we're surrounded with our loved ones, we want them to have everything that we want them to have, just as much as we want us to have what we want to have. So we go into the space of, "I can see them not wanting me to be as much as I've created to be." So it causes you to say, "I'll just put it on hold." And then you don't get to it.

Jen: *How many intentions do you think people have? Because we all have intentions for different parts of our lives. We've got them with partners, we have them for our job.*

I think most people want things to be a certain way, right? And how do you know that you're on your spiritual path that we always talk about in terms of intention, or not?

Janelle: I think one of the strongest areas that I see that most people want a big significant change in, like you said, either with work or with partnership, whether it's marriage or friendships or whatever. Those two areas are our highest. It's where we spend most of our time.

So it makes sense that we would want them to flow easier. These are where the issues come up with we look at either the person or the job as the problem. Instead of it's actually the lesson in it is for you. It's about you.

So the intention needs to be more directly about you. How can I feel happier with where I'm at? Because the thing is, you can leave the partner, you can leave the marriage, you can leave the job, but you'll get the lesson again.

Keith: *As many times as it's necessary for you to hear it.*

Janelle: And that's where you think the grass is always greener on the other side.

Jen: *What if it's the flip side? What if you are doing your intention and then you do get it? Do you just go out and give yourself a new intention?*

Janelle: Yes. We are creative beings. We thrive in vibration. So vibrational energy, our nature itself, is a malleable thing. It is changing in reflection to its environment. That's who we are.

We think of us as being solid, but we're not. We're vibrational energy, which is reflective of electromagnetic fields, thought processes, all the quantum fields that go into shaping your reality.

So everything that you experience in the world, the walls, the car, the money, whatever, is just energy. So if everything is that, then whatever intention you create, if you're also creating another paradigm underneath it, no doubt your world is going to be confused.

Jen: *I think that's sort of amazing. I think on one level we all know that we have that fear underneath us. Although I don't know how much anybody knows what effect it has on really stopping the intention from coming out.*

I know you've always said if you've got a fear you just have to go through it. Feel it, acknowledge it. Janelle, how do you know if you're on the right path to where you're supposed to be in creating what you're here to do? What spiritual lessons you are supposed to learn, who you are supposed to be?

Janelle: For me, at different points, I look at how uncomfortable I am. So if I'm extremely anxious or uneasy about something, there's something I need to move through there to get to the other side of whatever that is that's blocking me.

So it could come up that way. Or it could come up like this did with the technical difficulties and roadblocks that show up to stand in your way. Most people do the thing of, if I have five or six things that come up, I'm just going to give up.

It's too difficult. And in reality, the more that you push through that and understand that it doesn't matter. It doesn't matter that we had however many minutes of technical difficulties. That really doesn't matter.

It just matters how focused you are on the intention of what you wanted to create. Because that will get out there no matter what.

Jen: *I think a lot of times when we're thinking about creating our destiny, we almost feel like we can get there and then just coast. That's not it at all.*

What you're saying, when you come up against roadblock, when you're pushed out, almost into the water so to speak, and then you've got to rely more on spirit to help you get through and less on your comfort zone.

Janelle: That's not to say that once you get into the rhythm it doesn't get easier. Because it does. But it's all in perception. So if you perceive it as being challenging and difficult, then that's what you're going to get.

But if you perceive it as, "Okay, well this is just me pushing through something within myself to get me to wherever I need to be next, and this is great," then it will be more flowing.

And the more times those things come up, the easier it is for you to see whatever it is you need to learn through it. Sometimes it's religious stuff. Sometimes it's family stuff. Sometimes it's relationship stuff.

Like your husband may not be on board with what you're here to do. He may say, "I don't think that's possible. You can't do that. You have to be mom. You have to be this."

Or you yourself say, "I have to be mom. I can't do that." Which is easy for us to do as moms.

Jen: *I don't know how to work this in, because again my brain is still on nothing. All my systems are I don't know where (from the high vibration that occurred for the show to air). But you and I were talking this morning about how I recently had two people very close to me pass away in the last four months.*

One was semi expected and the other one was not expected at all. I was talking to you about going through some of their items after they passed away and realizing that there are so many facets of both of them that I didn't know.

And I learned a little bit about how many gifts we all have and what we share with people. And I don't know if you can talk a little bit about how that intermeshes with what we're here to do. Like the power of intention and creating your destiny.

For me it was not giving myself a chance to visit one of these people before they passed away. We just didn't know that he was going to pass. I realized afterwards there were so many parts of him that were gifts for the world that I didn't experience here with him because I procrastinated the time.

And I wanted to throw it out there in terms of intentions because I feel like it's an authenticity thing for people. Do we know who we want to be? Can we get through these barriers that you're talking about, whether they're easy barriers or not?

Can we be our authentic selves and share what we have to really give to other people because it was really special, both things from both people.

I was sort of sad that I didn't get to know that while they were here. I don't know if you want to talk about that.

Janelle: Well, for me, how it's been explained is that when you're here in this life you express as many talents and gifts as you possibly can with everyone.

And it's not about the income from expressing those gifts or money or whatever. It's not like you're supposed to have a job related to that. But the more times that we expand ourselves to realize, "I'm really great at this," or "I'm not so great at that, but it sure was fun trying."

The more times we can be comfortable with letting people see that and sharing our passions with other people, that gets cultivated in our family and gets cultivated in the people that we care about and that we share our lives with.

But we have been trained from very, very young to not live outside of the box that people place you in. It has served for centuries and centuries of time to fit into labels or whatever. But we're now at this kind of crossroads, call it the age of experience or whatever you want to call it, the shift, whatever, it doesn't matter. It's just that we are at this place where our soul is beckoning us and the universe is beckoning us to be more or to be fully expressed in the world.

So when you're with someone and they have crossed and it was a family member and you find out all these wonderful talents they had, sure the grief part of it is there because you missed an opportunity for them to share their highest self with you and their love and their passion. And that is a huge gift.

Like I said, it's not about the money end of it. It's just about, "I've learned that I'm a great singer." Like for me, a friend asked me to go paddle boarding. One, I had issues with water so sometime I have conundrums with that. I'm not a great swimmer. I was like, "I don't know how to balance. I don't know if I'm great at balance. But let's go try it." So we go try it. Get on the board, I'm great at it. I never fell off. I actually had better balance than my friend and she's like a kite surfer. I'm like, "Hey, yeah. I discovered a new talent."

So it's the call like, "That's great. I can share that now with people." And I'm free to share that about myself. But most people don't operate in the world like that. They have to be great at it. I don't care if I fall one hundred times. I just like the experience of trying something new. It doesn't matter. I just want the experience.

All of those things go into our intentions. So if you want to learn French, okay, go learn French. It doesn't matter if you're going to be a French teacher or going to travel to France. It may not be that. It may just be that your soul likes to learn new languages. It's just honoring that place within you. And being free enough with yourself to say, "I want to learn how to paint with water colors." Okay, well take a class. Or go buy some art supplies and try yourself if you don't want to take a class. Fine. Just try it.

Jen: *I'd like to read you a question that somebody emailed me about the show. A listener in New Jersey is trying to work on*

125

several intentions at the same time and she's trying to figure out if she's moving in the right direction.

These are her words. She said she keeps seeing repeating numbers. She's sending out an intention and then she keeps looking at the clock and seeing repeating numbers. She is asking how does she interpret them? Is this a message to tell her that she's on the right path for what her intentions are?

Janelle: Let's say you're writing down an intention and like she's saying, you look up and you see the clock and it says 1:11 or 1:23 or 3:33 or 4:44. Those are all angel numbers and also guide numbers letting you know that you are connected.

And what you're thinking about in that exact moment is what you need to look at. It's also about the intention, but what is your thought focused on?

Jen: *What if her thought is a fear? "I'm never going to get this done." That's their way of saying, "Stop. Yes you are. Turn it around. Pay attention."*

If it's a good thought, shift it and keep going. If it's not the best thought, get it out of your head.

Janelle: Right. Look at it. They are saying pay attention to this moment. Be present to this moment. Because what you're doing and thinking in this moment is of your highest intention.

Jen: *I think a lot of people, too, always want to know about the timeframe of their intentions. "I put out this intention, but then it just never happens. Why does one take longer than the other?"*

And again, it's what you're saying. We have to move it.

Janelle: We don't know. We put out the intention and we expect the universe and whoever is living on the other side to go bring it to us. And we don't do anything. We don't change anything. We don't take any action. We do not do anything.

We sit around and we go, "Well it's not happening." Well, yeah. Do something. Go after it. The fact of the matter is, whatever you want, whatever you need to create for yourself, it's up to you to do it. They will match you ten times the effort that you put in. But you have to put the effort in.

Keith: *On this show, we talk a lot about the universe and spirit, but to use a very common axiom, God helps those who help themselves.*

Janelle: It's so true. So true. In my practice alone I'll have people come to me and say, "It didn't happen." Well what did you change? Did you do anything to match the thing you're trying to create in your life?

Jen: *You have to take the step.*

Janelle: You have to take the step. And the truth is you really hold the power. You hold the power within you. You are the totality of the universe. Everything that you're seeking is available to you; every single idea.

And it wouldn't be yours if it wasn't available to you. It doesn't happen that way. They don't dangle carrots in front of our face to say, "Haha, that's funny."

Jen: *They give us technical difficulties here and there. Just kidding.*

127

Janelle: It's like, how much are you willing to get out of your own way and feel that pain and feel someone telling you one hundred times you're a failure to go after that, to create the life that you're wanting. How many times?

They'll wait one hundred times for someone to tell them, "It's yours. It's possible." Yeah, it's possible 110 times over. Go get it.

Jen: *I always forget that as infants, as babies, we have to learn how to crawl, to walk, to do this. And you and I were talking about the fact that we would get up, fall down, stand up, fall down. And that it wasn't until you got older that you started to tell yourself, "I can't do it. I can't do this or that."*

Our instinct was always to keep going, to keep moving, keep trying without even thinking. No baby ever thinks about it. They just get up and keep going. They just keep going and going and going.

Even a child that is trying to learn the monkey bars or something else, if you watch a kid that wants to get to know how to do something, they just keep doing it and doing it and doing it until it's done.

Keith: *At that young age, failure is not a point of reference.*

Janelle: Like you said, they don't have failure as a point.

Jen: *It's really true. They just do it. And much like what you're saying for us, they don't think falling down on the playground is a big deal. They're like, "Try again, try again." Until the sun goes down they're going to keep on keeping on, know what I mean?*

Janelle: You can say, "It's getting kind of dark here. Can we go in?" And they're like, "No."

Jen: *You and I had a conversation a couple weeks ago about when you do run into people who are not on your same wavelength and you can feel them not necessarily wanting you to shrink, but shrinking away from you. You said you were trying to hold the intention to love them back and I said, "It's not doing much." And you said also hold the intention for them that they find it, (their passion) depending on what it is. In my case, it was success for themselves.*

Janelle: The other thing, too, is that they're coming in your experience because either they are not doing something that they know they should be doing, or they're not being something they need to be. Or, they are feeling disconnected from themselves. Either that or there is something in you that is attracting that experience to you. So you have to look at all of those.

But it's about, usually, in my experience, because they're not willing to step into their whole self and take all of their opportunities and all of their consciousness or all of their things that are available to them.

Because they are judging you for doing what you're doing. Or looking at you like, "Why are you having so much success? Why are you having so much abundance? Why are you having so many opportunities?"

Because we live in a world where we have been trained not to live full out. Because if you do, then you must have something I don't have. I'm going to judge you for that.

So the more times that they judge you or come into that experience is less about you and more about them. Whenever I run into that it shows me how much on track I am. Not because I don't want them to succeed. It's actually that I am holding that intention so highly that everyone comes into the experience with me. They also get something from the universe for themselves.

Jen: *Hey, Janelle, you and I talked about this, this morning, how you have this ability to come up against these huge challenges and you just keep going.*

There comes a time in most people's lives where the ego takes over and they start saying, "I can't," or "I won't," or "I'm just sick of it." What do we do in those times? When you've had a life where you've been met with, or not even a whole life, but let's say a couple years, where it just seems like hardship, hardship, hardship. Let's say you flew through the first three, but then you get to like four, five and six and then you're like, "What do I do now?"

Janelle: I've had that.

Jen: *Because you do. What do we do in the middle of that?*

Janelle: You know, that's the running joke that people assume I just live this blissed out experience and that I don't have any roadblocks that show up.

Keith: *You mean you don't?*

Janelle: Just the other day, Jen and I were talking about this, I had a day jam packed with stuff. I was teaching a class. I had to be on the other side of Houston. I had scheduled myself to do meditation at night. I wanted to eat dinner with my family.

I got stuck in traffic, it was pouring down rain. I'm like, "Oh my goodness." I was late coming home. So I had to hurry up and eat dinner with my family, because that's hugely important that I have family time.

And I get to do the on-air segment and the internet won't work. The channel's not stopped. It took me probably fifteen minutes and I had to jump to another station to work it out.

I finally get live and the meditation that comes through was so profound that if I had not paid attention and looked at, "Do I still need to do this meditation? Do I still need to walk through this?" I could have let all of those things stop me.

Or in the case of just my life experience from being three and being kidnapped and going through that whole experience. I could have let that determine who I am. I could have let any number of my physical conditions—having a hemorrhage and having blood loss and all that and being in the hospital for two and a half months and not being able to move—I could have let that stop me.

None of those things have ever changed my perspective as far as going after what it is that I know I am called to do. I still get up and I actually look at life and I go, "You know what? It's actually pretty fun. Go figure."

That's my unique perspective of it. But I know that it's not the norm. I know that most people would take one of the experiences that I've had and totally relate to, "I can't go after what I need to do or want to do, because look at this. I have this. They're going to judge me because I was an addict. Or they're going to judge me because I have had three husbands," or whatever the case may be.

Those things, we all have issues. We all have things that we're less than proud of, decisions that we have made, even our fault. But those are not meant to be beacons that you base what you choose to go after in your life. They're not meant to be that.

Jen: *You always tell me, "You've got to wipe fear off your dashboard." And I think oftentimes if one of these barriers* happens to us we tend to label ourselves and then we can't move forward. Or you don't know where it started. It could have been a parent who said to you one day, "You're left-handed so you can't do this. You'll never play tennis," or whatever.

And I don't know what life would be like if we didn't label ourselves; so your words, "Wipe it off your dashboard," made total sense.

So, Janelle, I have one more person who emailed me about intention or really about destiny if you will, creating what they need. She is kicking around the idea of starting a business and she is wondering if that is what she is supposed to do, her next steps.

Janelle: Well, it is. That is what she is supposed to do. I would say she was supposed to start probably five or six months ago. It's not that she missed the mark, but I almost want to hurry her up and get her there.

So a couple of things that she needs to let go of is getting it right. I don't have that one. But a lot of people do. And the other one I would say would be being so overly conscious of details, meaning organization and stuff like that and letting that take up a lot of her energy and time.

The other thing is that really finally at the core of all these two top issues that I just discussed was, can she live outside of her family's identity of who she is supposed to be?

So that's the question she needs to ask herself. At what point did she identify with whomever, mom, dad, sister, brother, whomever, and it could be all of them, saying "You have to be this in our family situation or else there's going to be consequences."

Jen: *It's so interesting. For listeners, those are her barriers right now. These are the things. It's not necessarily that it's outside. It's* *in her head or struggle. Just sort of saying, "Can I do X? Can I do Y? And how do I do it?"*

Janelle: In the natural world, this is how it will show up and this is crazy cool. So it will show up like she goes to start the business and she gets on the internet and there's let's say fifty different ways that she could possible put an LLC together.

Well, so she gets bogged down by the details and she never gets off the first base. Or the other situation that happens is she'll share it with her family and they'll go, "Did you think about this? Did you think about that? What if this happens? What are you going to do if that happens?"

Jen: *Or a kid will get sick and they'll open up that piece.*

Janelle: Isn't that crazy cool? I say it's crazy cool, but that's how I view the world. So I just think it's phenomenal that what we're embodying in the cells and our DNA is actually sending out unconscious signals to the world that we live in to say, "Please bring me that reflection."

So that I can choose not to be what would make me ultimately happy.

Jen: *So in other words, if you're thinking, "I don't know if I can do it," that's what's going to be sent to you.*

Janelle: Reflected back to you. So you'll get, I don't know, you'll get roadblocks in the path, whatever those roadblocks are. Maybe her husband is looking at her like she has three heads. "How can you possibly do that? You don't have enough time."

Jen: *Janelle, okay, I'm going to throw it over to you just to wrap up.*

Janelle: So a couple of things we covered was if you're going after an intention, first you have to take an action. Take an action related to whatever that purpose is or the intention.

So you want to learn a new language, go sign yourself up for the class. Get the Rosetta Stone, whatever you want to do. But take an action so the universe can meet you. If there are roadblocks that come up, choose to walk through those places. If there is a fear that comes up, witness the fear and where it came from and what does it create within you. Does it create pain? Does it create sadness? Does it create disconnectedness and you just completely shut off? Some people freeze when they get to that point and they're like, "I don't know, I don't know, I don't know." You go into I don't know. Some people do that. You may oscillate between any number of those three.

And the other thing is to look at, "Is there something about your family that you may be identifying with? Like your mom didn't go after her dreams. Or your dad said that you can never be an artist because artists don't make any money." Where are those themes playing out for you in your reality? And then how much of your own stuff gets in your way? Like how many times you have failed, how many times you tried, and then you let those things get in your way as well.

So look at all three of those things consciously and don't get stuck by them. I am by all means telling you, please do not spend hours and hours and hours on this. This is not a place where you want to sit and just dive and dive and dive. Let it come up, look at it and move, move, move. Quickly. The other thing is to express yourself fully in this lifetime you have to share your gifts and talents with everyone. And you may not be a great singer, but you may need to sing. Just sing. Don't care what other people think about singing. Because the chances are, maybe they wanted to be a singer, too.

So that's it in a nutshell.

Show 7 – Intention Part I
Numerology perspective by Jen:
Life Path number 1

One energy is the perfect backdrop to this show because Janelle's Team shifted the energy and space around this show so we could learn about intentions earlier in the year than usual. We talk about this at the beginning of the show. The energy of the one is that of a leader and introducing new concepts to the world. Learning lessons so you can move on and create a new chapter. This was perfect for the topic at hand.

Show 8 – Intention Part 2: Facing Fears

Air date: November 18, 2013
Life Path number 8

Jen: *If you're tuning in to the show, whether it's today or three years from now in the Archives, that show is meant for you. You are meant to hear the message that we're telling you, or that we're going over. And that means you're ready to handle whatever Janelle and I are talking about that day.*

Last week we talked about the power of intention. Janelle went over three basic things to do when we set intentions. We need to take the action, and if we come up against a road block, to walk through it. If it's a fear-based roadblock, look at it.

And so, Janelle, how, exactly how do we walk through that fear and what's the lesson in the roadblock?

Once we're setting intentions and we're in the flow, what happens when people around us are not?

Janelle: Well, you know, part of it, part of the things that we've discussed, last week on Friday, was that we go and we set intentions, but oftentimes we find that we hit road blocks.

Or we don't, you know, we lose focus, or we don't follow through, or whatever those things are that sometimes they're not necessarily conscious to us. Or we're not aware of how we're stopping ourselves.

And, as you said, which I thought was such a great point, that little babies don't think about crawling or walking. They just get up and do it, and do it, and do it, and do it. Until they do it. And it's a great analogy for how we are born, that we still have that same energy.

We just have had failures and setbacks, so we relate to those things as we're chasing goals and setting intentions for ourselves. We let those things block us.

So, I think we should talk a little bit more about that and what are the subconscious patterning's and other people's limitations that we get kind of stuck in to. And how that shapes your intention and keeps you from moving forward.

Jen: *When I was listening to the playback, you said two things. You said oftentimes we'll set an intention, and either something, a road block will come up, whether that's another person or something external like traffic pops up. This can be what we end up focusing on or what can stop us from moving forward, because, in most cases, we all have an underlying fear of failure.*

I kept thinking, "What are we going to talk about this week on the show?" I thought we were done with the topic of intention but My Guides kept saying, "No, no, no, you're not done (with the topic of intention). No, no, no, nobody got it."

Janelle: We're not finished.

Jen: *I want to talk about this fear of failure. When do we all end up with failure? Because as you just said, we're not born that way. So when does that switch turn?*

When do memories of past failure become some kind of unconscious stream that we all play, when we go to do something new?

Janelle: Right. This is what they were bringing to me. So it's really quite—you'll find this really fascinating. So, here's what happens. You know like all babies are born with blue eyes?

Jen: *Yes.*

Janelle: Right, okay. So, it has a scientific reason for it, but the Universe's reason for it is because they're still connected with God. There's another fact in that. You know how babies are always born with a soft spot, where the skull hasn't closed up yet? That's actually another way that they are connected to God.

Jen: *Wow.*

Janelle: Right? So, two pieces, like, two pieces where the world hasn't shaped their reality yet. So, the minute that that skull starts closing, okay? And we get to learn from our experience through our parents, through our siblings, through friends at school, whatever. We learn, don't be this, don't do that, don't express yourself, don't be too loud. Don't, you know, be careful you're going to fall down. All of these things, right?

Jen: *Right, right.*

Janelle: And the further that we get away from that porthole being open, and with the being, the essence, the divine creation, and get more exposed to the phenomenon of the world, right? Because this place is a movable thing, that shapes your limitations. And you start looking at other people to demonstrate, okay, well, how are they living? I need to be like that. Or how are my parents doing it? Or how are my siblings doing it? And so that shapes the reality, which in turn gives you fears, limitations, experiences, failures, what have you. But in the beginning, you don't have that experience because you're just solidly connected with God. Fascinating, right?

Jen: *Totally fascinating, because—Do we even know when we start to lose that? Okay, because I'm assuming that most of us were good as kids.*

Janelle: You mean, we're not conscious of it.

Jen: *So we have no clue that we're sliding down the slide to a different reality than where we were. We're just trying to please other people.*

Janelle: No. No. (we are not conscious of it)

Jen: *Or make mom happy.*

Janelle: Right. Yes.

Jen: *Or got to play with sister so, okay, she wants me to do it this way, so I'm going to do it this way?*

Janelle: Right.

Jen: *And then that just keeps snowballing into a new way of who you are. Okay, but wait, Janelle, can we get back to that true one hundred percent connection? Is that ever possible for us to do, or to get close to that?*

Janelle: Not one hundred percent. We can get close.

Jen: *I guess you're right because then you wouldn't be here. Right?*

Janelle: Now, here's an interesting, I call these fun facts. The other interesting fun fact is every time I've been around someone and held their hand and helped them pray when crossing over, their eyes always turn blue. I've seen it time after time after time after time. And so you leave the same way you come in.

Jen: *Wow. I mean, it is like I don't say this small, but it is like tuning a radio. Like you're in that vibration.*

Janelle: Yes.

Jen: *And you talked about this last week, we are all vibrational beings.*

Janelle: We're all vibration. Yeah, this time period is meant to be for learning, that education. The fun. The playground. But we get stuck in, "I've got to get it right. I got to do this. I got to do that." Right? And less about paying attention to the essence, or the spirit that you are, that automatically knows where you need to be. And what you need to do. And what you were sent here to learn.

So, all of it, outside limitation and information bogs you down, but your intentions are the same as when you were younger. They don't change. That core piece of you is still the same. The same things make you happy, the same things that your soul knows, your gifts and talents, they're all the same. The only thing that changes is your reality of your world. The phenomenon. Existence. People, places and things.

Jen: *Okay, but when you bring that back, right? To trying to sort of set an intention, and I don't—I also want to go as specific as setting an intention, because what you just said was huge.*

You know, we're still there. What we are is there. And then all these other things come in, like fog around us. But…

Janelle: Yes, that's a great description. Yeah.

Jen: *But when it comes up, Janelle, is it coming up for a reason, then? Because, I mean, when we're a kid, and stuff comes up, I think a kid is more likely to flip back into who they are. They're going to say, "No, I don't really want to do that. I'm going to go over and play in the sand. See you later."*

Janelle: Right.

Jen: *"I want to play cars, right now. Good bye." As an adult, when a roadblock comes up, are they purposefully meant to come up for us to turn our vision back on ourselves and get our power back?*

Is that what we're doing with intention?

Janelle: Yes.

Jen: *What's the lesson, I guess, is what I'm asking?*

How can we figure out the lesson, instead of just calling it a roadblock, and then sitting on a side line and saying, "Nope, I always hit traffic, I'm never going to get there on time, forget it?"

Janelle: Well, okay, so here's the thing. You can sit there for hours and try to figure it out.

Jen: *Right. But you said don't do it, last week. You were like, no, no, no, no, no, no, no. Nobody gets in on this one, we're not going to therapy for this, people.*

Janelle: No, this is not where you spend your time. Because the basic fact is we need, there's stuff we need to do, your soul needs to express itself. And, you know, okay, great. You can spend hours and hours and hours, or you can quickly move through it.

You have the ability to quickly move through anything that you want, or you can choose just to spend years and years and years on one subject. But here's the thing. So, the basic rules of life. Either you're blocking yourself because you're afraid of failure.

Or because someone in your life knocked you when you got that place and said, "You can't do it. You can't do it." Or you stopped yourself. The other thing that we do is, if we get outside circumstances, like, traffic, the computer doesn't work. It's raining outside. Whatever. We use those as determining factors as to how successful we are. So we don't get there. Okay?

Jen: *Absolutely. We give our power over to outside circumstances. Right?*

Janelle: We do.

Jen: *For example, giving our power to the rain. If it rains again on Tuesday, it must not be right. Okay.*

Janelle: Yes, if it rains again on Tuesday, then this must not be right, okay. I'm stuck again.

Jen: *That's my vision from above. They're telling me not to do it. That's my sign. Okay, okay, okay, all right.*

Janelle: Like, if I gave you the laundry list of how many hoops I have to jump through on a given day, it's just the world. It's just the experience. It means nothing. It means nothing, and how... and how successful I am being at what I was sent here to do, it means nothing. It means nothing that, okay, the computer didn't work. I can make it mean something and say, "Oh, my God, you're stopping me from doing what I am supposed to do."

Yes, check in. Check in and make sure you're still on the right path. But don't make it like it's, "Oh, no." It's not. Follow the vibration. If your vibration is current and straight, the outside circumstances and the natural world do not determine what you are here to do.

What you're here to do is just trying to find God in your own internal life.

Jen: *Well, and that's the other thing, too.*

Janelle: You can't mess that up.

Jen: *Instead of blaming outside, we have to check in.*

Janelle: Right.

Jen: *And I think a lot of times the majority of us probably just don't even check in. We just write it off.*

Janelle: Maybe eighty-five percent. Write it off.

Jen: *Who is actually answering it?*

Janelle: You're answering yourself.

Jen: *Got it. So you're reflecting your own?*

Janelle: Yes. Yes, you're—when you put down an intention, let's say, "I want to create a happy, loving relationship." For myself. Okay, that's an intention, right?

So, if you experience roadblocks in creating that, then you have to look at what point were you creating that from. Are you creating it from the lack of having that? Okay. That's one constricted energy, okay? Because the truth is that you already have everything that you're asking for. So, that's one roadblock. The second one would be, "Well, you know, I've sucked at relationships about five or six times," so, you could have that consciousness in your thinking, not aware of it. But it's throwing out a fear roadblock.

And then the other underlying condition could be your family, or, let's say, religious convictions, right? Because that's a huge barrier for a lot of people that, you know, "I'm not supposed to ask for things that I deserve. I just need to be humble."

No, God wants you to have everything that you truly desire in life, as long as it's of the highest good and of the best intention for overall of the planet. If it's raising your vibration, and it's good for everyone.

Jen: *Right, and you're going to feel that.*

Janelle: You're going to feel it. You're going to resonate with it. You're going to feel it's going to resonate for you, it's going to, it's what I call pinging true. Pinging true, pinging true. You can't force an intention. You can't force an intention on your being that isn't true. How do you feel that? How you feel that you're forcing an intention on your life that isn't a true path for you? Because it feels constricted, it closes you up.

Jen: *Well, just like the feeling, I think, that you feel from family or from someone going against you, with an intention, it's the same. It's that awful feeling that it doesn't quite feel right.*

Janelle: Right.

Jen: *You can't go out and ask, "Can I win the lottery today?" No, it has to be, for the highest good of everybody. For your soul, for everybody else's soul.*

Janelle: Well, you can ask for that.

Jen: *Yeah, you can ask. Yes, you can.*

Janelle: I don't know what you're going to get.

But, you know, moving in to the higher vibrations and things is what, you know, when you're setting the intention. Okay, it's fine to just wish for, you know, on setting the intention that "I want to create a new job experience."

Okay. Well, that doesn't necessarily mean leaving the current job that you're in. It may mean that you need to speak the truth where you're at, and that is what is going to set your soul free, creating a new job experience.

Jen: *Okay, you have to say that again, because that was really cool.*

Janelle: Hello.

Jen: *All right, speaking the truth from where you're at, why? Because that puts you in your power and, again, it brings a truth to everybody else around you?*

Janelle: Yes. Yes.

Jen: *So once you free yourself, you can face it all.*

Janelle: Yes, because what you're always—right, yes. Because you're always, always, each individual soul, is always trying to raise their vibration and be the best that they can be. I don't care whether they're conscious of it or not, it doesn't matter. That doesn't matter.

I pay little or no attention to whether the person is actually consciously aware of what they're doing. Doesn't matter to me. Because the natural rhythm that is occurring on the planet right now is to raise your vibration.

Raise your consciousness to one of unconditional love of both yourself and your experience. Therefore, all of your intentions, once they are built in the reflection of who you actually are, and the unlimited potential and unlimited power that is within you.

You're born with that, you exist with that, and your journey in this life is to get back to that. Every single second of the day.

Jen: *All right, so now this makes sense to me, when you're saying if you're going to set an intention, and you're already in the fear mode, when you set it. You're not going to have smooth sailing.*

When you're setting an intention you need to remember where you came from, listen to the ping that says, "Yeah, this is what I want. This is really what I want, I don't care what so and so down the block says, I'm going to make time for it, I'm going to do it."

Janelle: Doesn't matter what your husband says. Doesn't matter what your kid says, doesn't matter what your husband says, doesn't matter what your sister says, it doesn't matter what your mom says. It doesn't even matter what you say, really. It really doesn't. Because when we actually just let go, and you just surrender to, "Holy crap, okay, I want to set the intention just today. Just one intention today. Like, how good could this day be?" Just try that one.

Jen: *Well, I even do it with my kids, I do, "Let's see if we can find a parking space," you know, and see how that goes.*

Janelle: Run with it.

Jen: *Just to practice, right, just to say, okay, let's just do it. Or "Let's just see if we can get downtown in two minutes, on through the six lights green," you know? Just simply to hold something. Once you say it, do you have to hold it? Or no? If you set it, and it pings and it's true, can you leave it? Are you supposed to leave it?*

Janelle: Well, timing is an issue.

Jen: *How does that work?*

Janelle: Yeah, you got to just, you got to own that, okay, so, like, a great example would be I have my house on the market, right? This is a great example. So, you know, my husband is relatively conscious, right? We have great conversations, but here's the thing.

So, this is great, I just remembered that I had this conversation with him yesterday. So, we have the house on the market, right? And we're showing it, and we don't, we already bought a piece of property somewhere else, so we don't want to float two notes, right?

That's totally reasonable, right? So, I said to him yesterday, because this is what occurred to me. It occurred to me that no matter how great my intentions were, and how true my energy was, he was blocking me with fear. Okay. So I said to him, in my wonderful self, I asked spirit, do I need to address this issue? They said, absolutely, because your high vibration is being met by—

147

and he's an extremely powerful man in himself. So we have two powerful energies, I'm sending out positive, and he's in fear, okay, well, that's negating each other.

Jen: *Right, then you get nothing, right? Or I don't know what you get. Whatever you get.*

Janelle: Nothing. A hodgepodge of experiences. One day it's going to be great, the next day it's going to totally suck. I could go in and say, "Well, then it's not right." I can go in and look at the circumstances and say, "Okay, well, this is, yes, we're not supposed to do this." But no, the current is yes. So, I looked at him yesterday, he's been gone all day at work. And I go, "Hey, you know, I really appreciate everything you're doing, it's great and I'm glad to see you, but can we work on this fear issue that you have around this whole endeavor?"

Jen: *Right. Was he open to it?*

Janelle: And he looks at me and goes, "Yeah." He goes, "Yeah. Right, let's do that. Perfect." I said, "Okay, here. Let's just work out this issue.

"How about you let go of the fear of working pay check to pay check, and not having anything to show for it, (the fear that) you've got to scrimp and save all your life to get something that you love? How about let's just let go of that?"

Jen: *Okay, so here's my question, though, since, Janelle, seriously, if we all just let go of that, then we do really create the space to move into. To create then what we need to get out there and create.*

Janelle: Yeah. Here's the thing. This is what I said to him. Yes, that's true. But what I said to him is, "You're not in control of the money. God is. You are God in action, okay? So why are you acting like a pauper?"

Jen: *Right.*

Janelle: That's not who he is. That's not who I see him as. But he's owning that frequency. As if, if he doesn't schlep it himself, it's not going to show up.

Jen: *Right, but if he...*

Janelle: And if he does, it's going to be really hard work.

Jen: *Right. Yup.*

Janelle: I'm not saying don't put in the work. But what I'm saying is, you've got to own who you are.

Jen: *Right.*

Janelle: And you're, each one of us is a divine essence of a holy creation. That's powerful in itself. Why limit it? So, that's what I did [with him].

Jen: *So was he even conscious of his fear going in, until you said that?*

Janelle: Yes. He said it.

Jen: *He was, okay.*

Janelle: Yeah, he was great with that. He said, "Yes. Yes, I'm willing to turn that loose."

Jen: *I'm laughing because I am to your husband who you are to my husband, in the sense of, I have the same thing with my husband. Just started this new venture, and I'm afraid—he's out there full on, full intention. And I'm wringing my hands going, "I hope this really works. I hope this really works," and not realizing, wait a second. Believe that it will work.*

Janelle: You're battling each other.

Jen: *Yeah, exactly. And that's really huge.*

Janelle: Happens in relationships all the time.

Jen: *So, I mean, that's humungous to know. Because you're supposed to be a partnership and honest to God, it never occurred to me. Even though, like, I try to be on point, try to tune in, try to use my intuition to do this, try to do that.*

How powerful we are, in partnership, anywhere, and it just never occurred to me how, in that instance, how powerful my fear can blend in with what we both set. So that's huge for setting intentions together. Holy cow.

Janelle: Yes, yes. This is—what's fascinating is, just in the moment, when you're saying that, they said, let's say you're not in a relationship with someone, okay? You're doing it alone (not in partnership), with it. So your relationship is with spirit. No different.

Jen: *Got it. Oh, my God, that's huge. That's huge. That's fantastic.*

Janelle: Spirit is holding the intention of unconditional, you can do it, you can do it, you can do it. This is possible, this is possible, this is possible. And you're being the fear.

Jen: *But this is fantastic, Janelle, and you just saying that, oh, my God, that's fantastic. Knowing that you got, I mean, the way that you said it to me is like, wow, we really do have a spiritual partner. You almost have like, the holding of the hands, right? Saying, you've got this. So, and I would assume, even if it's a partnership, then you've got the third person in there, kind of just being there. That's a fantastic way to look at it, though. The partnership with spirit, like, truly saying, "Go for it," right? "You've got it, get it, if you're out there."*

Janelle: Go for it, give it all you've got. Give it one hundred percent, we've got you. We got you. They do.

Jen: *And I think that's why you said last week, which I thought was cool, when the fear pops up, do not focus on it, get it out.*

Janelle: Face it. Okay, it's great, fine. We are all afraid. I get afraid. I mean, really. I have fears, you know, about different things, you know. A lot of people are saying, you know, because I'm up here in full out spirit mode, that I don't have fears. Holy crap, I do. Sometimes I have fears about being vulnerable with people, letting people see me. Because that's intense and maybe they'll judge me, or whatever. I walk through those places. But I'm walking through them quick.

And when I see it come up, I see it come up and I go, "Okay, this is my fear about being seen," or "That's my fear about being vulnerable," or "That's my fear about…" you know—because yesterday I had a fear about speaking to my husband about this fear he had.

Holy crap, yes. I had to call him out on his crap. Really? He's a man.

That's holding my power. That I'm also in the same sense, giving to him his power back.

Jen: *Why? Because you're letting him voice it?*

Janelle: They're doing the same thing with you, because every time they remind you, every time you get a nudge, this is still possible if you, that's them giving you your power back. But you just don't see it.

Jen: *Right, right. Again, we blame it (on outside circumstances) on the rain, we blame it on whatever, you know, what have you.*

Janelle: Right, stay the course. Stay the course. The timing is not an issue with the universe. Timing is an issue for us. We want it when we want it. We want it how we want it.

Jen: *So, well, and does that—and does that block it even more? Like, if we throw it out there and then we keep interfering and saying, "Okay, I wanted it yesterday where is it? Okay, I need it today, where is it?"*
Does that hold it up? Because those fears creep back in?

Janelle: Right. Right, and you're not—you're forgetting that there's a Master Creator, which is you. You are the Master Creator. So, maybe your higher self knows that there is a better, more fun option, that's in a better time frame. Just maybe.

Because time really doesn't exist for our higher self, or spirit or God, or whatever. That's just for here.

Jen: *Yeah, that's just this little thing they threw in.*

Janelle: Yeah, for our personal enjoyment, would you like this secret, too? Okay, great. Yeah. That would be fun. Then we go, I didn't, like you said, it didn't happen when I wanted it to happen.

Jen: *Right, and that's something you brought up last week, which is that lot of people go into either, I can't do it, or will others like what I do? And this creates a kind of brain overload, of thinking too much in their head. And I guess you would say, bring it up, let it go. And then let it go, right?*

Janelle: It might come up five or six times, I don't care. I don't care how many times my own fears come up. I really don't care. You know, and honestly. I tell you, honestly, from my standpoint, the more fear comes in my way, the more I look at it as a beacon for how close I actually am to moving through that fear. And see what's on the other side.

Jen: *So, okay, so the greater the fear, the closer you are to getting where you want to be. Is that what you mean?*

Janelle: Yeah.

Jen: *Because you're taking over, you're owning your power, so it's going to come back at you?*

Janelle: Yes.

Jen: *As in, oh, my God, I'm that vulnerable. Right? Got it, because you're that vulnerable. You're allowing yourself to be who you were. And again, when we were kids, we didn't care. I'm going to go sing in the rain, right now. Because I want to. What do I care? Right?*

Janelle: Right, who cares? Yeah, yeah, yeah. Right.

Jen: *And then as we get older we ask ourselves "what do I do?"*

Janelle: You create what other people see, and how they see you. And I'm going to look like a failure, and I really don't care. Fine. See me, yeah, I'm honest with my failures. Hell, yes. Look at them.

Jen: *Yes. Right, what I want to ask your Team, do they think that the listeners got it now? Like, what are they thinking? Because, this is huge.*

Janelle: I think absolutely.

Jen: *Yes, this is a half-hour discussion on how to break through the fear, and where it comes from. But Janelle, I loved, the partner and spirit piece. The fact that they're right there with you, you know.*

Janelle: Let Them Be.

Jen: *Okay, once we own our power, what happens? Which I think is slightly different than throwing up roadblocks. But when other people around us maybe aren't in their own light, and what happens when that happens?*

Janelle: Right.

Jen: *Because that—and also, too, you talked about last week, once you get comfortable, you do get into flow and then what happens to other people when we shine our light and they might not be where we're at.*

Janelle, do you want to just talk a little bit about what that feels like, or what that's like for you. And, you know, what flow means to you, I guess?

Janelle: Well, so, here's the thing. So we set out an intention, right? So, we'll just use your wanting to write a book. So, you want to write a book. You set that intention up. And then, so what happens is you have no idea where to begin. Okay, so then we've got to look at that. All right. So the rhythm happens when you start asking yourself, or asking spirit for help, right? So, you get the idea to write the book, but what we do is we just stop there.

Jen: *Oh, my God, we do.*

Janelle: Now, I want to write a book.

Jen: *You're totally right.*

Janelle: And then we wait for the universe to bring it to us.

Jen: *Right.*

Janelle: We don't ever go check back in and go, okay, guides, Team, higher self, I need assistance, or I need help with what that idea is. Give me help with that. Give me first steps.

Jen: *That would be what I would do, in the example of writing the book, I would say, well, I want to write this book, but I would have a conversation with my husband or a friend about it. And I have to believe, like, half the time I don't ever check in with spirit guides.*

Janelle: Right.

Jen: *I don't tune back in, unless I really need help. Then I say, "Help, what do I need to do?" Do you know what I mean? Like, that makes sense to me now, the way you're saying it now.*

Janelle: There's got to be a last straw, yes.

Jen: *Yeah, it has to be a conversation, and I would have never thought about it like that. Like, Spiritual Partnership.*

Janelle: It's ongoing conversation.

Jen: *So, talk, right?*

Janelle: That's flow. That's the flow. That's the rhythm, as it is an ongoing conversation, an ongoing check in. Am I still where I need to be? Do I need to move? Do I need to shift right? Do I need to look at this? Where do I need to be?

And be open to that it might take a winding path, to get to where you want to be. Just like in my case. Like, with the book situation, right? So, spirit drops in, it would be great to write a book about your life experience.

Yeah, that's great. But then they drop in, well, you know, we want you to get this other project done before you put that out there. And I'm trying to push the book. Not knowing that they have another project before they want to get the book out. That's staying attuned to the energy. I'm checking in. Checking in, I'm having this conversation. It's a conversation. It's not a daily thing, but I do check in. Where do you want me to be? Now if it's, you know, if it's a daily thing, like, you want to have more joy in your life that would be a daily check in.

Jen: *Well, not only that, a daily check in to the Universe, but also a daily check in to yourself.*

Janelle: Right.

Jen: *A lot of people may already throw up a barrier and say this. They may say, "Well, Janelle, you have the ongoing conversation, because you can hear your guides. I can't hear them." Right? Or, I can't do it, or, I don't know how to do it. I hear that all the time, from people. Where they don't know how. Or they say, well, they know how.*

Based on what we said at the beginning of the show, everybody knows how. We're not choosing to figure it out.

Janelle: Everybody has the same, yeah, they have the same abilities as I do. Everyone. We're born that way. That the only difference between me and someone who thinks that they can't connect is that I'm here to demonstrate what you're actually capable of. It's just being a teacher.

Jen: *And everybody is also here to have the experience then, in partnership. Like, just because you were not necessarily here to demonstrate, doesn't mean that the partnership isn't yours to have, right?*

Janelle: Right.

Jen: *Right, got it. Okay. Go ahead, go ahead.*

Janelle: It's an intimacy between you and spirit, you and God. That you forgot how to have.

Jen: *I like that you used the word intimacy. Because some people will say, they think that it's just some shout out message, right?*

For example, Janelle is just on the phone and her Team is going tell her turn left, turn right, go upstairs, you know, the way you hear your information is completely different, right?

Janelle: Right. So, sometimes, yeah, there's situations where they yell at me. Of course, just like in life, if you have a parent, you know, yeah. Don't go there. Or, you know, it's very subtle. They'll play a song. There's a message, for me. I'll be walking down the street, and you know, maybe one of the shops is playing music. And it's a particular phrase and if I wasn't paying attention, then I wouldn't have heard it.

Jen: *Go it, okay. Got it.*

Janelle: Then, you know, it's not necessarily me hearing, but it's me paying attention to the signs and the signals and all of that. You don't have to hear. You have to witness the world around you. Witness. Because just like in nature—

Jen: *See, that's huge too. Right?*

Janelle: Just like in nature, we are nature in ourselves, right? So, we have an automatic thing that is within you that says, grow with this time, grow with that time. Don't grow here. Don't grow. But we, in other words, through life, whatever happens, a set-back, a challenge, a time that's constricted energy, we look at it as a disconnection from spirit. When really, it's just the process of you evolving and growing into a greater connection.

Jen: *Right.*

Janelle: So fine tuning your intention for what it is that you're actually wanting, and here's the thing; most of the time, you're asking for things that are safe. And you still have fears around them.

Jen: *Right.*

Janelle: You're not even going for the big stuff.

Jen: *Wow. That's really huge.*

Janelle: You're not even going for the big stuff, you're going for the safe stuff, like, "I want a great relationship with someone who loves me." Or you know, but you're not really going for, "I would love to be a singer and produce my CDs."

Jen: *Well, and again, back to kids, that's why kids want to do five thousand things. They will tell you they want to do at least six things in their life, They will throw the ideas out there one by one and say "I want to do this", you know. And then "I have to get this", and" I want to do that, too", and I'm going to do it all at once. I think that they're so unlimited that they just, they're going to do it all at once. You know?*

Janelle: Right. Okay, yeah, that's why I use my example. I have five, you know, I have five hundred things going on at one time. How the heck do I get it all done? I can't even begin to tell you. I just know the spirit moves with me in such a way that I know, at the end of the day, when I lay my head down, my checklist is, did I live up to God's expectations of me, or the universe's expectations of me? Did I fulfill what I was sent here to do? And if I didn't, okay, I'll start again tomorrow.

Jen: *Well, tune in with the flow, I think if you get out of the way, from the fear, doesn't it get faster then? it is almost like a roller coaster, at least for me.*

Janelle: It gets faster.

Jen: *Like, for me it's like, when you realize the fear you had is not as great as you think it is. And so you step in to move through it quickly, then I really do feel like you get to the other side and it is an open space. It's freeing.*

Janelle: It's faster, the energy moves quicker.

Jen: *At the same time, I tend to look back and go, "Well, that really wasn't anything, why did I spend six months on that? What was I thinking?"*

Janelle: Right. Note to self, yeah.

Jen: *And the other thing about witness, too, is kids also are witness. They watch everything, at the same time as doing. But they watch and do at the same time. Like they're witness and moving. Witness and movement, witness and movement, witness and movement. Right?*

Janelle: That's what we're supposed to do, yes. Yes.

Jen: *So, and it does flow with them?*

Janelle: Yes, it does. We—it's meant to be an even exchange. You move, the spirit moves. You move, the spirit moves, you move, the spirit moves. It's always, you know, so once you get into that rhythm, you've seen it with me. It's moving fast. Quick, quick, quick, quick, quick, quick. Now on certain things, if you look at certain things, like with the book, it's moving according to their time.

Jen: *Right, right.*

Janelle: They have a destination. I don't know what it is. I'm not even concerned about it. But I was done.

Jen: *For the majority of people, and I don't want to put limitations on it, because here I am. I think most of us probably have one or two things going on, if we're not moving in a flow.*

Janelle: Well, so, here's the thing. Like, I'll just use the book as it keeps coming up. So, the book experience for me, right? I know that they have a certain time of when they're ready to release that. I've already seen the vision, I'm clear about that. Most people don't, can't see that, right? I'm aware of that. But so what happens is most people that get to the place of, okay, well, I've tried, I've written it, I've sent it to publishers, they're not accepting it, they stop. They stop trying.

Jen: *Right, right.*

Janelle: They stop trying, you know? They stop trying, they stop moving, they just let go of it altogether. And, that's what most people do. But what I find so fascinating is, so we can use my husband as an example, right?

Because he is, he would be what I would call, eighty percent of people, he's the majority, okay? So living with a majority person, it's helped me really understand how people do relate to their own lives.

So, let's say he's going after something. That he wants to do. He'll have the fears come up. He'll get stressed out. He tries to think about it, he lays in bed and he'll talk to me hours on end, you know. But I can't interrupt his journey, right? I have to let him have his moments.

And when he's expressing himself, I just hold this space like a listener, you know, I don't interrupt him. I let him have his a-ha, unless I'm supposed to intervene.

He will say, "I'm stressed out, I'm not getting enough sleep, I'm worried it's not going to work out," and I just let him vent. I just let him get it out. Instead of saying to him, "You shouldn't think like that. You shouldn't be like that."

I don't want to inhibit his light from shining, because that's actually his light expressing itself to me.

Jen: *Because once he gets, because those are his fears, right? So he's expressing all these things, he's eventually going to get to his power. He's going to relax and get back to where he needs to be, right? So it's almost like his way of re-aligning himself, right?*

Janelle: Yes. So, I look at that as the majority, right? He would be the majority, right? So he puts an intention out there. He wants to win a tournament. Let's just say, so he wants to win a tournament. So, he'll get really stressed out the night before, stay up, or wake up really, really early when he's not supposed to, and then just try to figure it all out. Okay. Well, then, let's say that he gets up in the morning and it's raining and it's storming. And he's like, "Oh, my gosh, it's not going to work," and all the things that he says. And I say, "Okay, well, can you do something else that might work?"

And then he may or may not win, whatever. And then he'll look at it like, okay, that's great; that was the experience. Some days he'll look at it and go, "I sucked at that." But the majority of the time he's learned from me that you just check it up as experience.

Jen: *Right, right.*

Janelle: It's the experience. That's it.

Jen: *But I think a lot of people don't realize that's just supposed to be what it is.*

Janelle: Yeah, it's just the experience. So when you set your intentions, it doesn't matter how big or how small. But, you know, so test the waters. Start with something small, and then have the conversation.

Am I still in the right place where I need to be? Am I still connecting the way that I need to connect? Is this good? Does this work? Does it feel right?

Jen: *Yes, and check in to see if you're still getting pinged, right? As you put it, right? Because if it feels right, if it's still the right way to go, you're actually going to be energized.*

Janelle: It will feel true, if there's fear there.

Jen: *You mean you're going to feel good? Or...*

Janelle: You can be, you can still be energized and still have the fear there.

Jen: *Really?*

Janelle: Yeah.

Jen: *All right, that actually makes sense. I get it in terms of me doing the radio show, of having to figure out the technical piece on my own (and still having a fear about it). I get that, totally. All right, I get it, I get it.*

Janelle: Yes.

Jen: *In my radio example you're conscious to what your fear is, but you're still moving through it, right, okay. Got it. So…*

Janelle: Yeah, you're a perfect example of that.

Jen: *I know. I built up a fear my head that I couldn't do it. I told myself, "I'm not technical." Well, that just shut everything down.*

I don't know where I got "I'm not technical." For all I know, I made it up in my head, and just decided to give my power away. And then I lived it for six months, instead of realizing it really doesn't take much to manage the technical piece. And you can throw yourself out there and own your power back and do it.

And that's not to say that Keith didn't give me a gift in helping me get on air, or anything like that. It just simply, when I look back at the experience and what I did to myself, I sort of think, "Oh, my gosh, that's ridiculous." You know, I can see how I built my fear up (doing the technical piece of the show, the sound and connection) to be much more than what it really was.

And that, yes, you can still have fear, but you can move through it and not let it put you on the sideline.

Janelle: Yes. And how free did you feel? Once you got it?

Jen: *Yes, I felt free. It was also really funny, I thought, I made such a big deal out of that? You know, it's not like 1978 or whenever,* *when there was a huge machine that was a computer the size of a room, you know. So, and I mean, you need a code to break in.*

Janelle: You might have had to be technical then.

Jen: *So then what happens when you do get into a flow and other people aren't?*

Sometimes you can feel their negativity towards you, or an indifference, or shift, in another direction. So what do you do when you finally do stand up and say, "Okay, I can do this." And you switch your vibration and you've got people around you reacting in different ways that you don't expect?

Janelle: I look at it as, when I meet resistance, you know, from other people, what I call resistance, it lets me know how empowered I'm living. It's almost, I look at it, again, like a beacon, I would say. To let me know how on track I am. Because the truth is, that most people do not allow themselves to shine.

Jen: *That makes sense, from fear, right?*

Janelle: Because—from fear, right. So when they see someone that is, their natural tendency is to bring you back into alignment with how they're living.

That's where you get judgment, criticism, what makes you think you can't do that. All of those things, that is because they secretly, this is how I look at it, they secretly want to be doing what you are doing, or living the way that you want to be living, that you're living. But they have no idea how to let themselves be free enough to do it.

Jen: *They don't know how to get there, right?*

Janelle: Right, right.

Jen: *With all those things that they put up in front of, it was probably, they put up a ton of barriers and they don't know how to break through them. And so, do you do anything for them, then? Do you send them love, send them success, send them this and that?*

Janelle: Yes, yes. Yeah, yeah.

Jen: *Because you know sometimes you can just distance yourself, right? And other times you can't.*

What if it's a co-worker and you've thrown out your intentions and you're doing really well, and your pieces or your projects are really getting out there and our co-worker is not. And so, if you're in the same office with them, you know, you're in that space.

Janelle: Sometimes they try to sabotage you, yeah. So when that comes up, you—that's the point where you, if it's a situation that's, you know, causing your power to be compromised, that's when you speak your truths. But if it's not a situation that's coming up where it's compromising your power, and it's just compromising the other person's power, I pretty much just stand in my truth. And I let them do whatever they want to do.

Jen: *In speaking your truth, depending on the circumstance, sometimes I've done things where somebody is maybe not kind or making me feel off, and I'll simply verbalize something like, "Man, are you having an okay day?"*

Because it just sort of seems like, or, "Is everything okay with you? You seem..." or half the time I don't have to go past that. People are going to say, "Oh, yeah, this is what's really going on."

Even though it's about a deeper issue, right? But do you find verbalizing the feeling helpful or not helpful?

Janelle: Well, I can't use my example, as myself, because for me, it's a whole other ball game. But I would say, it depends on the circumstance. Because if you have to judge the circumstance.

So, that's where you have to be discerning and see, if you're answering, if you're wanting to know, for the sake of making yourself feel better, that's a weakness.

And it's also weakness if you're asking the question for the other person to feel better. That's also weakness because it's people pleasing. So, if you have to be discerning as to why are you really wanting to ask that question. And is it beneficial to what is occurring in the moment.

Jen: *Okay, got it.*

Janelle: Okay, if the answer is, you know, good for the whole situation, then, yeah, ask the question. "Are you feeling, is there something going on with you," and if they say yes, then that's okay. That's fine, hold the space. But don't turn it into something about you.

Jen: *Right, okay.*

Janelle: Because, you know, that's why I say you can't use my example, because people automatically shift when dealing with me, whether I'm speaking about it or not, it doesn't matter. So, chances are, the thing is you have to remember that, yeah. That when you're, when someone is coming in to your experience, I don't care who it is, they've had a connection with you. You share something with them, at some point. I don't care if it's a negative, you still shared something with them.

And it's your job to figure out what. Because each person holds a piece of you and you hold a piece of them, it's there in your experience. Sometimes a greater piece, sometimes a lesser piece, but we all share pieces of each other. It's part of the deal, here. So, that's a huge part of it.

Jen: *Or whatever else your intent for them to... that would help them own their power back?*

Janelle: Right.

Jen: *Right. Okay.*

Janelle: Yeah, it's just a point where you shift it and make it about you that determines the situation.

Jen: *Yeah, that makes sense.*

Janelle: Because it may be about you, but you need to discern whether it is or not.

Jen: *Right. And again, so another reason to be checking in.*

Janelle: So, here's the thing, set as many intentions as you want. Set as many as you want. Cross off as much as you can. That's what we're here to do.

And you know, to have the joy of the experience. So okay, you want to run the marathon, what do you need, what steps do you need to take? Don't set the intention and expect the universe to bring it to you without even changing anything that you're doing in your current life.

You've got to change. You have to change. You have to put action steps in place. You can't sit around and just wait for it to happen, because it's not. That's a fact.

Do something. Get off your butt and do something. Do something that is different than what you're doing now. You want a relationship? Okay. Change where you're going to meet people. Change what you say.

Jen: *Right. Because when the road blocks come up...*

Janelle: You're vulnerable. Yeah.

Jen: *Yeah, look at them, yeah.*

Janelle: Look at them. Face them.

Jen: *Look at them for two seconds, or whatever it is, figure out where they're coming from, and keep going, right? And check in.*

Janelle: Keep going.

Jen: *Find out okay, this came up for me, what does this mean? Okay, all right, which side do I have to go down, how do I get to where I'm going, right?*

Janelle: Right. Be willing to be led, even if the path looks winding.

Jen: *Right, right. I love how you said that. How sometimes you have to go around. Sometimes you go around to get to where you got to go.*

Janelle: It's going straight and in circles.

Jen: *But you are moving forward.*

Janelle: You are moving forward. It may appear to you to be a circle, but it's actually not.

Jen: *Right, but you're moving. Well, I feel much better today, I think we really got it, this week, around. I don't know what your thoughts are but, you know.*

Janelle: I really feel it's solid, yeah. It's solid now.

Jen: *And like I said in the beginning of the show, if you are tuning in to this today, this is for you. Move, you know? Set your intentions, right? Do your thing. Be who you are, right? Yeah.*

Janelle: Yes, yes. With all, with everything that I am, if I accomplish nothing else in this lifetime other than to just empower you enough to say that every dream that you've ever had is completely available to you.

And to give you the self-realization that you can do it, that it is possible for you. It is possible. Every creation that you've ever wanted, from the time that you were little itty bitty and you could possibly dream about any kind of life, it's available for you.

Jen: *Yes, so put it out there.*

Janelle: And it is imperative to do it, to go after it, to make the attempt.

Jen: *Well, I like how you said before, dream big.*

Janelle: Do it. Why not?

Jen: *You know, get out there and go. Yeah.*

Janelle: What else do you have to do? What else? What else do you have to do that is so important?

Jen: *Well, and you did when you were a kid, right? We all dreamt big, we were kids, we all did. We all did, right? Yeah.*

Janelle: Well, be a fireman if you want to be a fireman, you know? On the weekends. Fun. Take karate if you want to take karate. I think I'm going to do that next. I want to take karate; I think it would be fun.

Jen: *I think you would be awesome at that. Oh, my God, it would be great. Watch out, you're going to be a black belt before you know it, right?*

Janelle: Yeah, I know, kick butt, right?

Jen: *Yeah, exactly. Exactly. So, all right, well, that's pretty cool. So believe it or not, we've spun through the hour. Do you want to take the last few minutes and talk about the Lunar Eclipse?*

Janelle: This weekend is also, today, is full moon. Not only that, it's an eclipse full moon.

Jen: *Yes, it's a Lunar Eclipse, yes. Talk to us about that, go ahead, tell me.*

Janelle: Okay, so it means, when you have an eclipse, it means bringing stuff, in a full moon, it means bringing stuff to the surface that is needing to be released.

But also, the ego is highly active during the full moon, so you may feel the need to express yourself. Do so in a constructive way, though. Speak your truth, but in a very heart centered way, is what this energy is about, this weekend. And remember, so it starts three days before, and it ends three days after. So we'll finish on Monday, with that energy, and just continue to release. Release, release, release, release, release, release. Which means, get out all your fears, write them down, burn them, throw them away, whatever. Don't create any new projects, just getting everything out. So, perfect time to do that.

Jen: *Yes, that's awesome, yeah, clear, like, clean the closet. Yeah, clean your spiritual and emotional closet.*

Janelle: Clear your closet, clear your space, yeah. You can see emotional stuff out of the way, please, please, please. So, you can begin to, on the full moon, take action steps.

Jen: *That's awesome. So, see, so all that fear? Get it out.*

Janelle: Yeah, perfect.

Jen: *Yes. All right, awesome.*

Janelle: And, as far as with me, you can reach me at janellehoyland.com. I'm on. See you next week.

Show 8 – Intention Part 2
Numerology perspective by Jen:
Life Path number 8

The traits associated with the number 8 are power and taking charge of your life. In this show Janelle showed us how to maneuver around our own roadblocks surrounding fear and the energy behind the show is reflective and allows us to turn inward to look at ourselves to get our power back.

Show 9 – Intention Part 3
Taking Action
Air Date: November 25, 2013
Life Path number 6

Jen: *Today we are talking again about intentions in part three of "Intentions." Janelle, are you there?*

Janelle: Yes, I'm here.

Jen: *Oh, I have no idea what's going through my brain.*

Janelle: You know, it's funny. Yes, I do.

Jen: *Yes, you do.*

Janelle: That's a spiritual joke.

I was thinking also, too, Round Three might be the charm. Maybe this third dose of intentions and getting moving on different things will get the ball rolling and put all the pieces together from the first and second show. If you haven't listened to those, please go back and do so, because like I said, this is the third show and the final piece in that intention field.

Jen: *Yes, and I thought that was going to be cool, because I was sitting here thinking to myself, "Oh, what do I want to talk about on the show?" and when I checked in with my guides, they were saying, "No, no. Nope, not done."*

I know you and I talked about this, but I was surprised. I was like, "Really? Really? Another show on intention? Okay." And Janelle, you had something to say about that in terms of the three, right? Wrapping up energy and all that stuff.

Janelle: Right. In the first show that we discussed, we explored how there are actually three parts to intention. There's your thoughts, there's your fears that are behind the thoughts, and then there's taking an action, right?

Jen: Yes.

Janelle: All three parts have to be in place, and so it's kind of like if you go in the series of stuff that we've talked about, the first show was your thoughts, and what if someone's standing in your way, and all of those things, and in the second show, we really dealt with the fears.

Now we're on the third show, which is about taking action. We kind of touched on that at the last show, about spiritual partnership and what that really means.

We take it for granted that we're actually working in a very evolved system that is set up for you to succeed, and it's up to you to step into that frequency of alignment and then maybe push through those things that are standing in your way.

Like with you, the interference of thinking that you couldn't do certain things by yourself, or like with me, thinking I'm the only one who can do it. I must get myself there. That's my barrier that I have to work through. The different things that we've put up in our way.

If you're working on intentions, one the intention is for you, so probably shopping it around to get validation for, "This is my dream. Don't you see my dream? Don't you like my dream?" is not going to work. I would say eighty-five percent of people don't go after their dreams, so if you're coming to them and saying, "Don't you believe in this?" they're probably going to look at you and go, "Stink Eye on it." It is important to have support, but if you're coming from the standpoint of shopping it to people, you can actually feel it before you even say it.

Jen: *You can feel the other person's... Their reaction.*

Janelle: If people are resonating with that.

Jen: *You can feel their reaction. Well, that's really interesting. So if you're actually going to go out and shop it around, start to tune in energetically around you, and kind of say, "Hmmm...Do I really want to ask my best friend if this is really the path that I should be taking? What do I really think they're going to say?"*

Janelle: Right, because they're going to have their own fears and judgments around that, because it may not be in alignment with their belief system.

Jen: *Your ship, your intentions.*

Janelle: They may believe that you can only be a mom. They may have a different set of belief systems, or they may have a whole set of fears that are blocking them. You don't know, so your job is to really stay in tune with that and listen, and pay attention to, "Are you sharing this with people that really are intending that you have the best life possible, whatever that is for you, and not having judgment towards that?" Or "Are you taking steps outside of your comfort zone to meet what the universe is asking you to go after?"

Jen: *Well, there it is.*

Janelle: Or "Are you just going for the small stuff?"

Jen: *Right, because what you just said now, "Is that person really behind you for..." and I forgot how you actually said it, "for all the* *great things you're intended to do in this lifetime?" How many people are put in front of us that really, that we have a partner or person that is in that place? But last week you were saying how spirit, or the universe, is that partner. Is that before anybody else, before anything else? They are the one and only shift, saying, "Yes, you can do it? Yes, go higher, go longer, go faster."*

Janelle: Yes, "Move. You can do it." It's unconditional love and support, is what it is, unconditional love and support, but we are so conditioned to look outside to people, to validate your dreams.

Jen: *You're totally right.*

Janelle: Because that's what we're trained to do that from the time we are very little. Think about it. Your kids come to you, and they say, "I'd like to be a fireman," and you go, "Well, yes, you can do that," or "No, you can't." Or, "I want to be a mom," or "I want to be a ballet dancer." It doesn't matter the ability of the child, right? That's their dream.

Jen: *Right.*

Janelle: Give them full force to do it, but we forget that the other partnership in it is spirit. That's set up for you from day one. That's how you dream in the first place.

Jen: *Right, that's your imagination.*

Janelle: Yeah. It's that little thing that you, when you're little, that's all you did. Now you go like, "Oh, I had a dream. Oh my God, that's amazing."

Jen: *Right. "Hey, I did that. Great."*

Janelle: You're like, "Really? Oh my God."

Jen: *It's that one thing.*

Janelle: Yeah, you need to get back to that original place of origin, which is being kind of youthful and childlike, and somewhat using your imagination, because that plays a role in it. If you're not open, which is just imagination, then you're going to limit your experience, so at any given moment, the universe is conspiring with you. It's your job to move into right harmony, or balance, or flow, with that, and not make anything up along the way, like some kind of random story about, "I had to jump over this hurdle. My computer shut down, and then I got sick so I can't do it, whatever."

Jen: *You and I talked about this yesterday, because I was saying, "I finally overcame a fear, and I was sort of going back into spinning mode," like I took one step, and then (I got fearful and) I'm spinning, spinning, spinning. I pushed a little more forward, and we talked about this, I think in the middle show.*

The last show, you talked about getting in the flow, and then, for me, on Wednesday, like everybody out there, I was so busy with (personal and family) things that I had to do, or things I thought I had to do—that I initially felt time-shortage and a real absence of flow. And then I had the experience of time literally expanding. It was like, "All right, okay, you're worried about doing x. You're afraid to do x. You took a step. Fine. Here, we're going to take a step for you."

What I mean by time expanding, in my case was, I had a laundry list of things to do, and you know, as a mom, you only have four hours to do a hundred things. And literally, I had more time than you'd ever know. It was as if time either stood still or really expanded. I got things done in a calm manner, and I got more done than I usually do on a regular day. I really felt like it was my guides saying, "There you go. We took that off your plate. Now get back to what we really need you to do." [laughs] How is it for you? Is that what you find goes on for people, or can go on for people?

Janelle: It can.

Jen: *Do people ever really get that they're in a flow, or do they just think they're having a good day?*

Janelle: Yeah, it really comes into that nonchalant kind of thing that we always do. We schlep it off to like, "Oh, I was really on my game today," or "Oh, yeah, it was a great day, but that's not the norm." It actually can be the norm. You're the best witness. That is the norm for my life. If you really logistically look at my life, there is no possible way that I get, in the normal time frame, there would be...It defies logic, the amount of stuff that I get done, and the amount of places that I am, and the amount of things that I do, because I'm here to really move a lot of things, and I know that if that's my agreement with spirit, and I'm moving in that rhythm, then they're going to move everything for me, which is what occurs.

So the trick is, at that moment, being so grateful for the experience of, "Thank you for supporting me and allowing me to move with spirit. Thank you for being so present with me and knowing that my schedule is tight today and giving me extra room. Thank you. I really appreciate you being considerate of the stuff," because they are, but you have to be allowing and be open to that.

Jen: *That's a huge step, but the other thing, too, is recognizing it, right, because I could feel it. I knew it was completely different than just a happy-go-lucky day. I was tuned into going, "Ah ha, I know what this is," because I knew I wasn't stepping forward. I was afraid, and I knew I needed to make a move to step forward, and so again, I tuned in, like what we talked about in the last two shows. Like you said in the beginning, stop asking around. Start tuning in, asking your guides, asking the universe, saying, "Okay, what do I do next? What's next?"*

So I say it's like for some people out there, it's just really recognizing and slowing down and saying, "Well, wait a second, where is that coming from?" What you were saying is, "Most of all, it's coming from your Team." Maybe through your Team, they said, "Okay, we're going to move this."

Janelle: Yeah. "We're going to give you all the green lights."

Jen: *You're right, and that day, people sort of stepped in and did things for me without me asking it. It was definitely a flow. I just think it was really interesting for me, because I knew exactly what it was, but I don't know how many people actually tune in and say, "Okay, there it is." Like you said, if you recognize it and then are thankful for it...*

Janelle: And grateful.

Jen: *Yes, or grateful, just keep going and going.*

Janelle: Yeah, you get more of it, and then it becomes not a moment, but it becomes a life.

Jen: *I was going to say, it becomes your life, Janelle.*

Janelle: Yeah. You can use that example, it's fine.

Jen: *Yeah, it becomes a flow.*

Janelle: It doesn't mean that there's not things that come up, because there's stuff that comes up all the time. That's the life that we live in, is a phenomenon-based life. It's based on things that we experience, but they're not actually tangibly real experiences in the sense of the bigger picture. The bigger picture of it, when you cross over to the other side, you're not going to get this huge epiphany about the five lanes that you crossed over to get through the red light, and then somebody was walking down the street holding a sign. All of that's a blur. That just gets wiped.

What matters is how many steps did you take towards your highest intention, or your best life possible? That matters. How well did you listen? How much did you set yourself free, beyond your limitations, labels, and everything else that you put on top of you to make you fit into the box as normal?

Jen: *Right.*

Janelle: Whatever the normal is. It doesn't matter

How much do you box yourself in, in and around other people to make them feel comfortable?

Jen: *Right, that's huge. You and I talk about this all the time. I don't know if I'm saying the right words, but making yourself less, not shining, because the other person might not be able to shine theirs, you don't want to outshine them, blah, blah, blah, and really if you are shining or doing what you are supposed to do, don't you then boost them?*

Janelle: Yeah, it's a dance. It's actually kind of a dance. At a certain point, what happens is it becomes an even exchange. They see you, you see them. It becomes a dance of the soul between two people. It's a beautiful thing. It becomes a rhythm, and so that is the same with, when I say "spiritual partnership," it's the same thing. It's just you're working with a thing that you can't see, necessarily. That's when you have to get into the dance or the rhythm with spirit in allowing the universe to meet you at that with the amount of effort you put in.

If you're sitting there going, "I want the universe to bring me a great relationship," but you're not moving off your butt to do anything or change anything, or look at yourself in any way, shape, or form, but you're still doing the same thing, you're not going to get your needs met, because you're not moving.

You have to move. You have to move, and you have to let go of expectations at the same time. It's crazy business. [laughs]

Jen: *That's huge, too, because again, I think we want it done the way we want it. We're like, "Well, I want to meet the guy in the red shirt. That's who I want to meet. I want to meet that guy over there in the red shirt, on the corner, at 5 o'clock on the 17th."*

Janelle: "And I want him to give me a big kiss, and then he has the ring in his pocket. We go get in his private jet, and then we go, "Woohoo," for the next 40 years." Whatever. We put all these expectations around it, and so we limit what the universe can actually bring us. What they can bring us is more than you ever thought possible. Your vision, your dream of what you want is limited.

Jen: *I think you have to give our listeners some kind of insight for how to handle times when we catch ourselves in the limitations, how do we undo it? How do we shift?*

Janelle: It looks like this. "I am letting go of all expectations of what I think it should be, in order for the universe to exceed and meet me at where I'm at."

Jen: *That's huge, and it's easy to just say, "Let go. Let go of the expectations."*

Janelle: It's not easy, though, because think about it. Our whole entire being loves to hang on to every part of our experience. We like to hang on to our thoughts, we like to hang on to our fear, we like to hang on to our body, we like our complaints. We are creatures of habit. We like to hang on to what we know.

If you push the boundaries of what you know, that's where the whole field opens up, the playground begins.

Jen: *This is a crazy question, but are our guides frustrated with us when we get so close, or we try twice, and we just need to try three more times for something?*

Janelle: And give up.

Jen: *Are they like, "Ugh, now I've got to figure how I'm going to bring this back into their field of vision over here. How are they going to learn this lesson over there?"*

Janelle: No, they're infinitely patient. One of my favorite things is—like with relationships. Let's say you've been married for a long period of time, and there's this certain theme that's replayed throughout that relationship, a certain lesson for you. You throw up your hands. You go, "Oh, well, it's the other person. They suck. They're not getting it. They're not getting me, nah nah nah nah nah." Sometimes that's the case, if it's an abusive situation or whatever.

What I'm saying is usually that lesson will come back around if you get into another relationship. They never lose patience. They'll always bring it around to you. It's just how many times do you want the same experience? I don't know. I don't.

Jen: *Me, too. One and done. I want to be done with that.*

Janelle: We have a lot of resistance. The thing, too, is your bucket list, or your dream list, or your manifestation list, is really not even close to what the universe wants you to experience. It's like one percent.

Jen: *You said this last week. You were like, "Guys, you're not even going after the big stuff."*

Janelle: Yes, you're not going after the big stuff. No, not at all, because the big stuff is really scary.

Jen: *Is it that we think that the big stuff is going to create that much more work and no flow? What is it that we think? Or we just don't even put it on our radar? Because we're just so used to going small, small, small, small.*

Janelle: Right. Here's the other thing, too, is you may put the one that you think is a big thing, let's just say. You think it's a big thing, and you could go, "Oh my God, that would never happen in a million years," and then you never take any action towards it, because you already have the mindset that, "Oh my God, that's never going to happen." You've already set yourself up from the beginning to not have it, or not be it, or not do it, and the other thing, too, is, we also go with the thing of, "Well, if I have that big thing, then I can't possibly have this," whatever it is, like a happy family, let's say.

Jen: *Yes, you're right.*

Janelle: We always think something has to give in order for the other thing to be great.

Jen: *You're totally right. That's actually huge. You're absolutely right. You put up there on the screen, "Here's what I think I want to do." Intuitively, "This is what I want," and then you go, "No, no, no, no, no, because then if I do this, then that will happen, and that will happen, and that will happen."*

Janelle: Right. Like, "My kids will be missing me too much and be resentful. They'll be crabby, and I won't be an effective mom, because I'm going after—I want to be a spiritual leader."

"I can't possibly do that because it's going to take too much time away from my family." Well, what if one could support the other? Then actually doing what you're called to do is going to give you more time to be with your family. Hello?

Jen: *Right, and again, I think really, Janelle, people have to, when they start to really do that list that pings with them that we talked about last week, like, "How do you know if you're doing what you're supposed to be doing?" It feels right.*

When you take that step and you realize you pushed through that fear, then you start to get that flow. I don't want to call it the payback, but that is the pushback. That's that flow that then you can say, "Okay, I get it. I can do it again."

Again, what we said at the beginning of the show, time really does expand.

Janelle: It does.

Jen: *I think it's hard to see it, or hard to think about it, if you haven't felt it, or felt it, but hadn't realized what it was.*

Janelle: Totally. I was thinking what they were bringing to me, is when you're making your list or you're thinking about your "best possible" or "this would be fun" list. Really, when I say "ping," you can actually feel it in your body, is the truth.

For those that are kind of disconnected from the body, then you can say it out loud, and if it frightens you, okay. I'm not worried about that, but if you feel it expand your body like it makes you take a breath, that's what I look for. That's a good, general rule of thumb. If it makes you hold your breath or constrict, that's usually fear. I'm not as concerned about that, but if it's not really what you want to do, it's not even going to hit your body's radar, meaning it's going to be somewhere in left field. Your body's going to be like, "Eh, not feeling it." Generally, it's usually somebody else's idea or implant that they've put on you.

Jen: *Generally, then everything that comes into your radar is definitely something you can do, could do? There should be no limits, no anything on what we can do? Universally, you can do that on a Tuesday with your eyes closed. That's no problem.*

Janelle: Exactly. We go, "I don't know." That's our favorite phrase when you put something on the list. "I don't know how to get there. I used to know how to do that."

Jen: *And also, this just popped into my head. What do you think about this? Money. People are going to go, "I can't do that. I can't afford that," or, "I can't, or this will—If I quit my job to do this, then I won't be able to fund that," or whatever.*

Do you find that that gets in the way of people or not so much?

Janelle: Tremendously, and really, money is just energy. It's the same thing as flow. Really, money is just about how much can you receive? It's just a tangible tool that we use in this life to validate how well we're doing or how not well we're doing.

Jen: *Right, but we do that. "We," right?*

Janelle: We do that. If you just understand that money is just energy, and how much respect you have for energy will allow you to have more flow and rhythm with it.

Jen: *So if you know that your life is flowing, flowing, flowing, everything in your life is going to flow, no matter what it is— friendships, money.*

Janelle: Right, love, money, health, it's all the same.

Jen: *Green lights.*

Janelle: It's all the same. It doesn't matter.

Jen: *A beer at the bar, a seat, a parking space, whatever, there's going to be more abundance in everything if you're in the flow.*

Janelle: Exactly. Now you've got it. This really is how the universe looks at Earth and the world and our lives. This is the playground. That's how they describe it to me, any time they can. This is the playground. Anything and everything is movable that you see in your world.

So just think about that for a second. That includes illness, struggles, whatever. Whatever is in this reality as an experience, whether it's a tangible experience like a car, money, whatever, or an illness, it's all movable.

Jen: *I just had somebody text me. A listener from New Jersey is asking about visualization. Lots of people talk about visualizing or seeing yourself doing or having what you want. Is that limiting?*

She's asking, "How do you visualize without limiting?" I guess is the question, and, "Is visualizing a good tool, or should we believe? Does it play into this at all?"

Janelle: Visualizing is an extremely appropriate process and very valid in this experience, if you're going after something. Here's the thing—because visualization is focus, but what we tend to do is, we just—for the example, let's say you're going after a new job.

You just focus on getting the new job. That's all you focus on. You don't focus on what it's going to look like, how much money you're going to make. Any of those things, you leave out. You just focus on getting the new job. Then you get the new job, and then you're not making what you need to make, and the people there are having all kinds of friction with you.

Jen: *Then that circles you back to the partnership with the spirit where you go back to unlimiting.*

Janelle: Focus on the intention of, "I'd like a new experience with working, whether that's a new job, or however the universe defines that. I would like a new experience with that."

"I would enjoy making more money." Focus on what that would look like. If it's a job that you're happy in and you enjoy, focus on the feelings associated with you being there and having that. So less about the details of this amount of money, this amount of benefits, this particular company, but more about the feelings that you're feeling related to the experience. That's the visualization.

Can you see yourself there? Can you feel yourself there? is more important. It's pushing beyond that just being something that you see in your mind, like, "Oh, that would be great," into actually feeling it in yourself and your DNA.

Jen: *Yes, because again, I really do believe all this stuff about intention. I think we're so much in our head, myself included. I have to push myself out of my head, especially me.*

So I do really think you're right. Everything really is about feel, feel and flow. If you feel it, can you flow?

Janelle: Because feelings are vibrations that people have.

Jen: *Anyway, I know we're almost to the end of the show. I don't know if you want to wrap up with anything you have going on in Houston.*

Janelle: I do. I'm extremely grateful for one, for you, Jen, for taking your time aside from your family every Friday to bring this to everyone, take all the callers and walk through your fears of trying to figure out the technical piece of the radio show.

I've just been super-impressed with that, and I just had to let you know, because I always express how I feel with people. You know me, with you. I just am extremely grateful for everything that you do.

I'm grateful for the callers that called in and their willingness to be open and vulnerable with their lives, with people that they don't know. Thanks for that, too.

Jen: *Same to you, Janelle. You know how grateful I am to you. I love how you put this yesterday, how this show is an evolving conscious shift, which is exactly what it is. We want to get it out there to people, to lift them up to their highest good and know that they've got a partnership in that.*

And with Janelle, you know it's always going to be fun. I mean, come on. If you know her, especially, but I'm so grateful, and I'm really grateful for the callers, and for all the people listening.

Funny moments by Janelle

As the show happened, unfolded, on more than one occasion I found myself in weird awkward moments doing the show. The lesson I learned from that is I can do the show from anywhere. Several times was when I had to travel for a family vacation, I had to do the show wherever I was. Here you go; imagine this test. I am in the middle of four thousand acres of Texas desert hill country on the border of Mexico. No internet tower. No heat. I had a make shift antenna to connect to the nearest tower. It is about thirty miles per an hour wind. I have to drive up a mountain to get range for service on my phone. The vehicle is a 4-wheel drive 4 passenger ATV. Umm. No roads. It is around forty degrees outside. I sit in the cold bundled up as best as I can. I do the show, freezing wind howling, dedicated. Then head back down to the camp; it's about thirty minutes because it's so rugged.

Sometimes I could not control where I was when we had a show to do. My hubby likes to keep me on my toes. So, true to this whole journey, many times I was in awkward positions while having conversations with Jen. One of those shows was on relationship and marriage while my husband and kids were in the car. It never failed. I always had a plan to be in my office, but on key shows I would be with him. Oh, well, he probably heard way too much about women and women's empowerment. He would sigh, but he was literally the driver at that point so it was really a true test. Could I stay connected and present to what needed to come through me in the middle of compete external turmoil? Could I pass the test? During that car ride we covered topics such as clothes, how to date your husband, and how to remain connected even though you are growing at different rates. He never once talked to me about it after. He acted like the whole thing never happened. Too funny.

 ### Show 9 – Intention Part 3
Numerology perspective by Jen:
Life Path number 6

The energy surrounding the number 6 is home and family. This is perfect for this show because we talked about the Partnership with Spirit we have when we set intentions. Janelle reminded us to get back to our original way of thinking and viewing the world. We need to come together and view each other as one family.

CHAPTER FOUR
DIVINE MARTINI
"GETTING CLEAR"

Show 10 – Fear, Untruths We Tell Ourselves
Show 11 – Getting Clear

Show 10 – Fear, Untruths We Tell Ourselves
Air Date: November 1, 2013
Life Path number 9

Jen: *This week, we're actually going to be talking about fear again. And how we can sometimes manifest fear in ourselves using all kinds of untruths about ourselves. All these little ideas and thoughts about ourselves that we think are true that are sometimes negative or all the negative talk that rolls around in our head.*

Janelle has been teaching Spiritual Boot Camp in Houston for a special group of people for the last couple of months. The class is open to everyone. She is beginning to teach Spiritual Boot Camp Two and her Team literally just told her to tell me to tell you guys that this Saturday's class will focus on how to understand your Team better.

I just said to Janelle off air, "Can you please take that out on the road?" I scream to my Team, "Speak up guys! Come on, I can't hear you."

Janelle, I know you want to say something about that. Let's hear your thoughts before we talk about our message for today. Because clearly your Team thinks we need to hear from them so we can figure out the message for today.

Janelle: As you and I often talk about, with me it's so much of a flowing conversation at this point. Because I'm so attuned to what needs to come through in the moment—they were definitely adamant about how we need to work in harmony. Kind of going on that theme that we finished out last show which was about having a spiritual partnership. The thing is, that's great and all, but if you don't know what your Team or your partners in spirit feel like or how to even address them, because different people have different things.

I like to work with everybody on the spiritual side. I'm not discriminatory in that sense. I like them all. The more the better. But there are quite a few people that just work in forced groups. Certain people that just work with angels and that's what they're here to do.

There are some people that are here to work with the earth elements. And then there are some people that connect with harmonic energy. And then there are people who connect with angels. There are helpers on the other side for technical help and this is one for you, Jen. I'm glad we brought that up.

You need to understand that you do have a technical crew on the other side. So you might want to stop trying to figure that one out yourself and just ask them to assist you. "I'm going to ask my spiritual tech support Team to assist me in this endeavor at this moment, because clearly I need assistance and I'm willing and open to you."

Jen: *Just so the listeners know what happens to me when I experience technical difficulties--I freak out. I end up shouting in frustration which effectively blocks me from any kind of connection. Now just note that whenever I do any tech for the radio or any tech for a client or any tech for anything, I'm always invoking my guides, the angels who I tend to work with, the helpers always from above but I block assistance with my frustration and fear.*

Although today, Janelle, I have to share with you I did receive messages today. Once I stopped holding my breath.

So in a moment of breathing the answer did get to me. And it was actually quite easy and I found what I was supposed to find. But in the two minutes before that, it was debris, debris, debris all around the room in terms of my thoughts of frustration and my holding my breath, which is not the flow. Not at all.

Go ahead. I think it's really cool that we all have the ability to go to anybody at any time and not limit ourselves to one group. But I also find it interesting that some of us do just want to come in and work with one group.

Janelle: Right. The thing is, since the universe considers this the playground, which we need to actually understand that. We consider it work instead of being the playground. What I mean is being on earth they consider to be the playground. That's because anything and everything we could possibly need, want or desire or dream of is cultivated here. And then also in addition to that, everything is movable and pliable. So that goes with your Team as well. When you invoke them, when you ask them for certain assistance, like today I was driving in the car and my Team popped up. My guides said, "You might want to ask for a group of people to help with communication with a certain person." Okay, that's fabulous. Because sometimes we have trouble working with communication with certain folks. I'm like, "Sure. All right, I'll add that to my box of to-do lists for my helpers on the other side"

I have assistants and guides that help me open certain doors that might be previously closed to me. So, the thing is in the moment when you were holding your breath, we do that, we freak out and we cuss or do whatever. It's not about the fact that you don't do that or you choose not to do that.

It's how quickly can you move through it to get to the other side of what you need to get to. You got that, right?

Jen: *I got that today. What was amazing is I was like, "Oh, it's right here."*

Janelle: It was right in front of you the whole time.

Jen: *It was. It was on the right-hand side of the screen. Right there.*

Janelle: And so what we do when we hold our breath, we block the flow, the rhythm, because breath is the universe, which is your guides, which is their Team, which is your spiritual partnership. So that's why you hear me periodically when I've spouted a lot of spiritual concepts at people, I ask them to take a breath so you can download some of that information. And I know at this point I've kind of figured out the spirits around me in the sense of mode of operation. When they're channeling something through, it often is faster-paced than I normally speak in.

So I've caught little glimpses of that happening in my reality.

So once I feel my speech kind of raising, you have to understand when we hear guides it's a radio frequency that we're tapping into. Much the same as dogs when they hear a whistle. It's a higher octave that's inaudible to the human ear, unless your ear has been trained to hear it. Well, how do you train your ears to hear it? You tune in and you tune in and tune in and tune in and disassociate from the outside external noise until you get to that higher octave where they can speak to you.

In the same sense, they're speaking at light speed, which is very quick. So that's why when you meditate, you get a message and when you get out of meditation you try to write it down and it takes you forever to figure out what the heck was said to you so that you can write it down.

Jen: *They answer every single question we ask, right? So if you're driving in the car and you have a question and you ask that, it is answered, right?*

Janelle: Right, but it's not going to be in the same time frame.

Jen: *Okay, that was my next question. Is the answer in real time? Or are they like, "No, sorry, she's driving. You're not going to get that right now."*

Janelle: There's different variables. If you're asking the question, but say it's a really triggered emotional question for you, then you may not be able to receive it at that moment. Or it could be the flip and they know that you really need it at the moment then they can pop it in. It kind of depends on the circumstances and where you are at in your journey. But also how open and receptive are you to that might not be the answer you wanted.

Jen: *The answer you want, absolutely.*

Janelle: And quite often, like I didn't ask for this particular Team of helpers to help me with communication with a certain person. I was like, "We're good. I'll just roll with that on my own. "But also they apparently thought I needed it.

Jen: *Was that in real time, too?*

Janelle: Yes.

Jen: *Oh, it was? Because I was going to say maybe that was something for you that was like five months ago and they were just saying, "By the way, here it is."*

Janelle: No. They popped it in. I didn't ask for it. I didn't ask for help with that. It was something that wasn't registering on my radar as a concern. But at this point with me, they know they have total freedom with me to drop in whatever they need to drop in. That's going to assist me, because that's what I put out there.

Jen: *So for us that are here, I have a bunch of questions. Number one, I know you said we can have an infinite number of people in our Team, right? So that said, there is no one in particular that we necessarily need to say, "Let me ask this person or that person." We can just put it out there.*

And also, how do we know? I've had people ask me this question numerous times. They'll say to me, "Okay, I'm putting it out there. How do I know when I get it back?"

And I know you just talked about frequency and breathing and slowing down to hear it and that it's not coming in audible to the ear. But oftentimes for me, and you can tell me one way or another, I'll get a thought.

Not every time, but a lot of the time I'll say, "That's got to be from my Team." Does it come in as a thought for everyone?

Janelle: No, not everyone. Sometimes they're feelings. That's why the best way I can describe it to you is it doesn't feel like you. You can tell. It is something that the core of it, the resonance of it or the essence of it itself feels totally different than what you would normally think about.

It's a statement that wouldn't normally cross your field. So that's the best way I can describe it to you: how does it feel? You know what you sound like. You know what you think. You know what you talk to yourself like. We're an expert in us. We're good at that. But when you start getting to the guides and the angels and that frequency, a lot of people make the assumption that when I hear it or I'm receiving information that it sounds like me. It doesn't. It feels like someone else.

Jen: *And if it's not the answer they want, they may dismiss it and say, "Well, that's not what I wanted to hear."*

For lack of a better word, are Our Guides standing in roll call every day and we're getting like five percent, three percent of what's coming through?

Janelle: That's why I try to stress this, why you hear me say it so much: this is the playground. We are in this world, the tangible earth, is a frequency. It's a vibration.

So if you're standing there and they have however many helpers you can possibly imagine on the other side waiting to help you and you ask a question but you're disconnected from being open to the outcome for the suggestion they have on the other side, well then they're going to stop talking.

Jen: *How long does it take the typical person to figure out that they're disconnected?*

Janelle: It's a real quick assessment. What I say is, "All right, what's your outlook on life? Are you depressed? Are you feeling melancholy on it? Do you get up in the morning and look at yourself and actually see yourself?" That's how you know.

Jen: *Right. Or are you just rolling through the stuff, "Here we go again."*

Janelle: Right. It doesn't mean that I don't have periods of that. Like the other day, I spent like a whole week doing that and I was like, "Okay, I'm not present at all. What am I doing? Why am I disconnected? This sucks. I hate this."

Jen: *So we have a caller. You know what I want to do with this caller, if we have the caller's permission, Janelle, tell me if we can do this. I would love to not only answer this caller's question that they called in with to listen from the show, but also to see if this caller is in touch with their Team.*

Let me know if we can do that before we move onto today's topic. And if the caller is willing.

Janelle: Yes, we can.

Jen: *The caller's not willing, because they just got off the call. Sorry, caller. I was so hoping for a caller.*

Because people always ask me, "I don't hear my Team. I never hear my Team." And you know, Janelle, I struggle with the same thing. Of course I do.

But I know that you know my issues with my Team because you know me so well. So you can't really use me as the Team person per se, or maybe you can. We kind of did that at the beginning of the show.

If anyone is out there that's listening that would like to, just call in with a question. Or call in and see if you can hear your Team and hear your guides. The listener number is 347-XXX-XXXX.

And I find this amazing that your Team brought it in, because our whole topic today is all the other stuff that goes on in our head that probably blocks anything that's pure and light trying to come from our Team.

And the other thing too, Janelle, that I want to talk about at some point, and I'm only throwing it out there now so I don't forget, is how much our Team probably talks to us in our sleep or right before we wake up. And do they make up for lost ground at night time? I know I've said this before, but we are actually more open at night for some of us than we are during the day.

So do we want to talk a little bit about all the other mumbo-jumbo in our head that blocks our receptivity to our Team?

Janelle: So what occurred to me last week, I was doing an exercise in my lovely spiritual boot camp class. You all just have no idea how brave these ladies are. You have to understand, if you're signing up for boot camp with me, you'd better put on your boots. Just saying. Because it's no holds barred. The gloves are off with spirit. And not only are they off with spirit, but they allow the people that are listening to see me so clearly and so tangibly. That in itself can sometimes shake people up, as Jen can probably attest. Being with me in a close environment definitely shakes your whole paradigm up.

So what we ran into was we needed to do a surprise task with them and that surprise task I knew going into it was going to push their buttons. And the task was they needed to go and wear a sign out in public about this new thing that I'm doing called Free Hugs. And we went through, "I'm going to get arrested. I'm going to get my picture taken, it's going to be on TV. The news crews are going to be there. My family is going to see this," to everything else you can possible throw in the mix.

Okay, so I'm standing there and the spirit says to me, "Give them the option. All this monotony of mental funk is coming out. Give them the option. They can choose to not wear the sign and go, or they can wear the sign and go. Give them the option."

So I did. So three of the four ladies wore it. Four ladies went. And we had a beautiful exchange. None of the stuff that they worried about actually occurred.

What did occur was that they began to see different things with their own world shifting, how people responded to them. How certain people were open to them, X, Y and Z, all those things that happened. None of the things that they made up actually did happen. Not to mention that they were forgetting that this is my home city. This is where I live. This is where I take my kids to school. My kids know kids. Let's just say they forgot to think about me leading the class. People might not be open to that. So off we went in the caravan of free hugs out on a sunny Saturday.

They wore heels and they were all dressed up. I didn't bring them sunscreen and that was part of it. I should have told them to wear flats. That was also part of it.

Was spirit ever interested in any of that? No. And what they got from it was a huge shift in how they perceived the world around them. How they perceived everyday people. Because what occurred was people would look at the sign and you could tell that it was a mark just on their being. Being so open and so vulnerable actually triggered people's defense. They felt violated.

Jen: *Like, "What do you mean, free hug? What do you want from me?"*

Janelle: Why are you being out in the world? Who are you? Who gives you the right to do that? Why are you walking over here next to me? I don't want to read that sign. Why are you carrying that sign?

It wasn't that they were saying it, but you could feel those words in the air coming from the person. It was amazing. Then the other thing that happened was the kids would run from a mile down the road, running to us, open arms, jumping on us, celebrating with us. Just an all-out expression of spirit.

Jen: *"Free hugs! Yay, somebody gets me! I hug all the time!"*

Janelle: That was the deal. And then the other question is, why are you doing it? We didn't have an agenda. There was nothing hidden. There was no agenda. It was just about changing and shifting the energy. That's it.

So we spent probably forty-five minutes giving out free hugs. Let me tell you how much time we spent on mental crap: an hour and a half.

Jen: *And that's with you. That's with Janelle as the leader, which is kind of amazing. You're such a high vibration and all these ladies are, too. So it's like, "Holy cow." And again, here we are blocking the Team.*

Janelle: Totally. And I'm watching it go down. I'm watching it unfold. We also dealt with blocks in the sense of cultural blocks.

I have one lady who's in the class and culturally they don't hug. They're not a hugging culture. They don't do that in their culture.

There are a lot of things we were dealing with on a global scale. That's with four ladies. Well, five including myself. Not only that, my husband, I love him to death, but he looks at me and says, "You're just going to let random dudes walk up to you and hug you?" So then I had to clear up that one. That was about all aspects coming together. It was really about shaping and shifting the energy. Now what happened was we finished out the time together. I went and took them to lunch. We went to lunch and they said I scared them on the drive over there.

Jen: *Like, "Where is she taking us now?"*

Janelle: No, my driving scared them.

Jen: *I love your driving actually.*

Janelle: It's a time warp. Then we had lunch and we put the signs on the back of our chairs outside because we were sitting outside by the water. We put the signs facing outward so people could walk by and read them. They would stand there and read the sign and not say anything, just standing there with blank looks on their faces. They wouldn't say anything. It was crazy, I'm telling you.

Jen: *Would you engage them or would you just let them stand? What would you do?*

Janelle: I would just let them stand there at that point. For me, that's why I give you the example of I could actually see the energy and the thought coming out of people as we would approach them.

Jen: *That's exactly what I was going to ask you. So we have all these thoughts in our head like, "Oh my god they're going to think I'm crazy. They're going to take pictures of me. I'm going to turn red."*

And then vibrationally, you can see this. Not everyone can see this. What did that look like? Do you see aura shifting for some people? Is it like you're suddenly a rainbow and now you're gray? What does it look like?

Janelle: So let's use the example of the person who had the assault on their being. That is such a heavy, thick vibration. It really doesn't have any color. It's just thick. So if you were to take, the best example I can give you would be water and like pudding. The thought and all of that was such a thick vibration. That's why I could discern between that and what is around us at any given moment. Because it was so thick. It wasn't a color. It was just thick.

Jen: *The feeling, right. And that's what we do to ourselves all the time then.*

Janelle: Right. Imagine if you're walking around with how many thoughts you have one day, it's going to be millions. I'm not saying I'm immune. You can imagine. It's on a bigger scale so I have to do a lot more work. And so if that thick energy is there, it's no wonder your Team has a hard time getting through to you. You can't hear them.

Jen: *There's no way. They're walking through pudding. There's no way.*

Janelle: Yeah, you're taking something that is just in essence pure energy, like electricity, and trying to move it through pudding.

Jen: *Move it through mud. I get it now.*

Janelle: They're going to get through because they're determined. You're not. They are.

Jen: *That's why for me even today, the whole thing at the beginning of the show, I'm telling you I lost the screen of the show right before I was connecting to Janelle. And I called the wrong person. But I wasn't breathing.*

So there was mud and in the breath I got the answer. But I had to breathe. I had to breathe. Janelle, it's interesting with you because I have known you for a long time now. And when we're on the phone just regularly having a conversation and you start to channel something in, you do breathe quite a bit.

I can hear that you're trying to catch up to them. I can hear a really deep breath in and out. It's so interesting because there it is, downloading, downloading, downloading.

Janelle: And sometimes, like this weekend just to use that example, I'm doing the meet-and-greet with your Team. What will happen is since I have to bring in their Team more clearly for them and then in addition use my Team at the same time, well you can imagine I have to take a lot of oxygen in. Oxygen and breathing expands your capacity to receive. And so what will happen is because I have attuned myself to being so open with the breath and flowing with that, I'll have to take more in.

Jen: *That makes sense. Is this why for some people when they exercise they can hear, too? Because you're doing something else;*

you're kind of clearing your space and you're getting in a lot of oxygen? So if you're a runner, a lot of runners will say, "I tune in a lot right after I'm done running. I find my answer."

Janelle: It's that, but also when you're moving your body, it frees up the minefield, the programs of what you put into place. It frees that space up so then you can connect more.

Jen: *That's fantastic. We are almost out of time for the show today. Can you give listeners some information about how to contact you?*

Janelle: You can find me on Facebook, which is Janelle Hoyland. It's also JanelleHoyland.com. On twitter it's @janellehoyland. I'm all over the place. YouTube, you can find some videos, meditations and what not. And then I will be doing some travelling. I've come to Jersey how many times? Like three or four times.

Jen: *I was just thinking about you because last year at this time you were preparing to come.*

Janelle: It was right after Hurricane Sandy.

Jen: *I don't know what I was doing. I said to myself, "Last year you were five days away from arriving." Jersey needs you some more. Or maybe I just need you. One of the two.*

Janelle: It's always on my radar.

Jen: *I know you're doing boot camp again. Did you already say that? Boot camp two.*

Janelle: We're in the middle. So we're on the third class which is meet and greet your Team. And then the fourth class which is crazy bad. When I say bad I mean intense. It's holy communion with holy spirit. So we'll see what rolls out as a result. So these are not recorded. However, they happen is however they happen. We can't reproduce them in any way, shape or form. You know me, I love serving and I love sharing. I offer my heart. Have a great weekend.

Show 10 – Fear, Untruths We Tell Ourselves
Numerology Perspective by Jen
Life Path number 9

A repeat energy with 9 being about surrender and wrapping up of lessons as well as allowing ourselves to surrender. In this show Janelle reminds us that we need to take action to get what we want and once we do that it is possible to move into a rhythm with the Universe and just like a dance we will get into a flow of creating what we really want in our lives. My favorite quote from this show is Janelle giving us a prayer to help us surrender or step out of the way so the Universe can step in to help us "I am letting go of all expectations of what I think it should be in order for the Universe to exceed and meet me where I'm at"

Show 11 – Getting Clear
Air Date: November 15, 2013
Life Path number 5

Jen: *Good afternoon and welcome to Spiritual Happy Hour.*

Today we are talking about your vibrational output and how to protect your own space, and what that means.

Anyway, Janelle, how's it going today? Did you ride your bike?

Janelle: No, not today. We played outside early this morning, and it's nice here. It's back up to eighty degrees so we're enjoying the flip flops and the weather, as we were at thirty-five degrees and now we're at eighty. That's how it goes here.

Jen: *Yes, it's crazy.*

Janelle: There's so much energy and so many things happening on our planet right now. You can just see it in all of the things we've had occur over the last, you know, three, four years really. There's been a lot of influx of energy as we go through this what I call revolution into living authentically on this planet and really cherishing it as a gift and doing what we're called to do, and expressing our love freely. With that comes our own personal challenges, right?

Jen: *Oh, gosh, yes.*

Janelle: You know, the truth is, most people that are walking around that are somewhat conscious are really highly evolved spiritual beings who decided, like you actually decided, that your life and your gift would be most beneficial on the planet this time so you chose to reincarnate and bless the population with your loving gifts and talents. You're actually here to discover what those are. Then that means you got to work through all of the layers that you consider adult. That's why I call it the playground.

Jen: *Yes, because you got to play. If you don't play and let loose, then it's not going to be as much fun.*

Janelle: No, even working through your own little stuff, too, you know, you got to treat it as a gift. Thank God I am going through a situation right now because I know something is going to happen as a result that is beneficial to my being.

Jen: *I think that's really huge because as you said, so many of us are going through so many things on a global level, on a personal level and there's a lot of hardship going on for people. I think it's really huge to remind people again. We keep talking about this show after show after show that as you just said, as these things happen to people, that they have to not take a step back but they have to kind of keep going and much like you just said, realize that there's more to it. There's something behind it, sort of how to dig deep, right.*

Janelle: Right. You know, as you, I'm not immune to personal challenges. Mine are just on a little bit different scale, you know, incorporate a lot of different elements. We are here to discover what our connections are to each other.

What is your soul's intention in this life? Sometimes that's not a big huge worldwide movement. Sometimes it's just to be a great mom and to really enjoy that. That might be an aspect of your soul's purpose here.

Jen: *Right. It's interesting because before every single show, I sit down and meditate and try to figure out, okay, what spirit wants me to bring through for the show for the highest good of everybody. Janelle, I'm sure you do the same. Then you and I talk whenever we connect each week. You'll say to me, "What do you want to do for the show?" I'll throw out my ideas. Then you'll say your ideas.*

We'll sort of come to something. I'm usually always coming off of whatever I learned from the last show. In the last show that we did, we talked about connecting to your guides. As you remember, we weren't really supposed to talk about that but two seconds before the show aired, I had technical issues.

I just couldn't hear anything or any of what my guides were trying to tell me. I'm certain that they were shouting at me but that said, I have walked through the last couple weeks trying to create space and trying to be more mindful, more quiet so that I can hear whatever frequencies are coming through for the highest good for whatever is going on in my life.

As we move towards the end of the year, I sort of turned around the other day. I know I said this to you, Janelle. I said, "Oh my gosh, we're almost to the end of the year." I was thinking to myself, "Thank God spirit let us do those intention shows four weeks ago because of the vibrational push I feel to get things done by the end of the year."

There are so many more family obligations going on for me right now and I am trying to stay focused on my spiritual do to list and my intentions right now. But I feel the pressure or push from family obligations now so I don't know that I could have been clear and calm enough to do the shows on intention at this time of the year. You would have had to do a lot of grounding for me to be able to do that intention show now. My point is I sort of stumbled upon really trying to protect my space, protect the integrity of the intentions that I threw out there, and really get in touch with what that vibrationally feels like.

I just find it fascinating that once you get on a roll, if you will, with an intention, there really is a space. There really is a space out there for your intention. Like I said, I just felt the need to really think, "Oh my gosh, I've got to protect this. I've got to figure out what is of the highest good for this thing."

Anyway, I find that fascinating how you had said, depending on what you're here to do, your intention for this lifetime, for this journey—or many of them. It may not always be what you think it is, but you have to have attention towards it or be paying attention to it.

Janelle: What my Team is saying to me is that it's an intentional focus that you're focused on; it is a spiritual focus, spiritual focus on, okay, this is my moment where I'm going to work on writing a book.

You're giving yourself an hour to do so or two hours of that time window. Now here's the thing. Everything will probably come up in your world to stop you from doing said activity. That's just reality. That's life.

Being concentrated and being focused on what it is that you want to accomplish in that space is protecting your spiritual environment so to speak and your soul's purpose. Actually it's really clearing for the body because then it's not worried about the five hundred gazillion things that it comes up with in your mind as to why you don't need to sit down and do whatever it is you need to do or take action on it. When, in fact, when you do so, it actually frees up your heart and your solar plexus which is the divine life force called the divine figure eight that runs through us.

When you begin to move in that flow and that rhythm and that harmony, then that's what creates stories and openings that weren't available to you because you didn't have the spiritual focus and resolution to follow through with what you know that you should be doing.

Jen: *Now here's my question. It's the end of the year, and toward every end of the year, does our spiritual self try to wake us up to, "Hey, come on, now you've put it off for yet another year. You know, get moving, get moving." Right?*

Janelle: Right, because the vibration that occurs during that timeframe is with every single person, they go, "Oh okay, well now I need to create a new life." That's the vibration, okay? That's what's set and then we go, "Oh yes, that sounds great. I'm going to just write down or think about all of the things that I would love to do in my life." Well, then you just go back to living your regular life as you've done every year in the past without taking any further action towards what it is that you really, really want to achieve or what your intention was in the first place.

It's basically just writing something down on the paper is my thought.

Jen: *Yes, also we've got so much pressure from outside sources like the media, holiday shopping, this and that. It's a wonder anyone can think.*

Janelle: The thing that I love most and they were bringing this in was that I don't have the time.

Jen: *To shop?*

Janelle: No, I don't have the time to meditate, I don't have the time to sit down and write my book, I don't have the time to work out, I don't have the time to eat right. I don't have the time to whatever it is you can come with behind. I don't have the time.

Jen: *Oh, you mean everybody else is saying, "I don't have the time." Exactly, "I don't have the time." That's the thing though, Janelle. This is what I think we have to talk about, too, is because what I've been finding out is I may start with five minutes.*

Okay, the kids are watching TV or something is going on. I'm just going to take five minutes. I'll say to them, "It takes five minutes to meditate." I usually turn around and it's never five minutes. It actually ends up being twenty, twenty-five, you know, a little bit longer because once you do really settle down, I find that the time expands or things get taken care of around me.

You know, I'm not 9-1-1. Nobody necessarily needs me. The house quiets down. I've found that there actually is more time but once you have to sit down to actually start.

Janelle: Right. That's you moving in the rhythm with spirit because when you're honoring that system like I was talking about before, that spiritual focus, when you say, "Okay, I'm going to sit down. I'm going to sit down at this time every day, and I'm going to sit for 10 minutes," or whatever, however long you set for yourself, the spirit knows when you're going to show up. It has that in its appointment book.

Jen: *Wait, what? Spirit is waiting for you?*

Janelle: Yes.

Jen: *Can you say that again because I think our listeners need to really hear that? All of us need to hear that. They're waiting for you? They have their popcorn. They're ready to go.*

Janelle: They have their own agenda; their own appointment book.

Jen: *Are they totally saying, "Oh, thank god, so-and-so is sitting down again."*

Janelle: Yes, they do.

Jen: *In that regard too, I've got to tell you because we talked about this a couple of days ago, I set the intention that I really had to get a lot done for the show. There are a couple of things that you and I want to get done and I needed to get it done. Lo and behold, two play dates popped up for both kids. I took two kids to school. One normally comes home with me. Guess what? He got a play date on the playground at school for the rest of the morning, so my morning was now free, good to go. But I got home, and you know this, Janelle. Phone rang, doorbell rang. Other people I wanted to connect with, it's almost like they vibrationally felt like, "Uh-oh, she's free, ding, ding, ding." I didn't shut them down.*

I had enough time, but I told you this on the phone. It was amazing to me that it seemed like vibrationally, because these people had no idea I was free but the phone rang. It was like fifty-five different things in my—I don't know what you want to call it—that weren't on my agenda, literally knocking at the door, physically showing up.

I was kind of chuckling going, "What the heck is going on here?" I do think spirit cleared the space. Then I feel like, as I said to you yesterday, it was like a test or whatever. I feel like the space was clear. From a vibrational standpoint, I feel like other people were like, "Oh, she's free. Let me pop in." Can you talk a little bit about that?

Janelle: Part of it is, yes, it is a little bit of a test. But here's the thing, the world, this keeps going. The world doesn't stop because you cleared your calendar. It's your choice.

It's not that you can't take the phone call but it is your choice at that moment. That's again about that spiritual focus. Okay, that person needed you at that moment. That's fine, clear it, be done with it, and go but if you go into the space of—here's the catch— "Holy crap, get away from me, you're depleting my time, I cannot focus on you. Just get away," what the universe is asking you to do is to allow those things to occur but still remain focused on what it is that you actually want to do.

The truth is that they can create as much time as you need.

Jen: *That I believe because again, I've seen it done in my own life. I've been there. I have been in a traffic jam and have gotten places much faster than I normally would have, green lights, that kind of thing (and that is the Universe expanding time for me). So, if someone comes into your space when you are trying to accomplish something of your own you just need to let them talk or vent if they need you?*

Janelle: And make sure you don't go into the lower vibration because that's the deal. We're never going to be in a world that phenomenon doesn't exist, just reality because the third dimensional reality, there's stuff happening all the time. It's just frequency stuff.

This is happening over here, and this is happening over there. It's much like ADD. If you let it distract you, then yes, you'll never get anything done but if you let it come into your experience, "Okay, I dealt with that, let me move on and then refocus," then you will train your environment to shift around what it is that you need to get done.

Jen: *When you say environment, do you mean the people around you from a vibrational standpoint? Do you mean that in other words, it's all going to happen anyway but as you just said, it will happen not necessarily faster but there will be more time created? Even if you have to stop off at three different stops before you get what you need to be get done, you'll still have the time on the other side. Is that what you mean?*

Janelle: Right. Also what I mean by environment, I mean things also, emotions, things, people, everything in this natural world is environment that can keep you locked into the theory that you don't have enough time. Any person that has been around me for half a second will know that I don't move in the construct of time. I don't. Whatever the case may be, but I get a lot of stuff done, a lot, magnitudes of stuff, both here in the natural world and spiritually, what my folks want me to create.

Jen: *A lot of people think they get stuff done but it's not the stuff like what we always say. It's not the spiritual stuff. It's not the agenda stuff. Right?*

Janelle: Yes, it has to be both at this point. It has to be what fulfills. Okay, so I'm riding my bike yesterday. I made the decision in the morning when I got up. I said, "You know, it's kind of breezy today. What does my soul want to do? My soul wants to ride him (my son) to school on my bike. Okay, that's six miles total."

My body goes, "You know Janelle, it's cold. He's going to be cold. You don't have enough time to do that." But that's what my soul wanted to do so there was a debate. My body didn't want to go but my spirit was so happy that I went, and I did it again. He's bee bopping with the birds, talking to his school busses, having this little plethora of spirit air. I picked him up again from school. I took him. It's about twelve miles. That's two hours out of my day technically but I got everything done I needed to do. There was nothing missing in my day and I got to have a great conversation with spirit on my bike.

Jen: *That's what I wanted to say to you as well, because we talked on the last show about being open and hearing spirit, hearing your guides. You actually said to me, too, "Once you hold the space, it creates more space and creates a platform for it to be where you can actually hear them."*

Again, it's so interesting to me that you're sort of saying your spirit wanted to do one thing, your body wanted to do another. How many times does that happen to the rest of us? Probably a million, trillion times but we just go with the body. We're like, "No, it's raining, sorry, can't."

Janelle: Yes.

Jen: *Again, can you explain how the messages can come across for us in what kind of way?*

Janelle: Like yesterday—I'll just use yesterday because it's a great example—when I was having the debate about the body and what my spirit wanted to do, it's not like I ride a bike everyday twelve miles, no. But that's what my body needed.

What happened was there were two things. My body was clear in its rebellion against what my spirit wanted to do. Even while I was on the bike, the debate was occurring because my body was saying, "Just call Steve," my husband, "and tell him to pick you up."

My spirit was like, "Uh, no, we're enjoying this bike ride. This is what we're doing." It's a layer of vibration. I just listened to the body. I said, "I know you're tired. It's fine. That's all right. We're going to continue with the conversation."

I was thanking my body for serving me. I was thanking my body for its heartbeat. I was thanking my body for its breath, and that my knees work, and that my feet work, and my eyes move and my brain thinks, and my arms move, and that I can actually ride a bike, you know. I just started doing all the thank yous. Finally, it just shut up and I finished my bike ride.

Jen: *I was going to say, did it come in line?*

Janelle: Yes, it just wanted attention is what it wanted, right? Then I finished. What occurs with spirit is that we hear little nudges. They're little subtle things like, "That might be fun," or "Take that class," or "Go talk to that person," or "Go turn left."

We ignore it but it's really the natural progression of things that we're supposed to be listening more. When you hear that come up, when you speak it out loud, I hear you telling me to turn left. That's why you hear me often say to my Team or my guys, or my angels or whatever I'm working with at that moment says this. This is what they're saying. They know that I'm speaking out loud. I then have the choice as to whether or not I'm going to choose to do what they're asking me to do.

Jen: *That's huge because it's so funny, I forgot you had told me this I think the other day to speak it out loud because again, it reinforces to them that you're listening, right?*

Janelle: Right.

Jen: *Then I suppose you put it in your own being and then you say, "I heard," right? It must resonate vibrationally with you that much more. It's solid in you then ready for the next step, if you will.*

Janelle: Right, because your own voice, too, which is your vibration that you're putting out in the world is huge. When you hear it back, that's even better. When you say, "I'm hearing," or you can even say, "I'm feeling," or "My heart says," or "My Team says," or whatever. It doesn't matter as long as you express it. Then at that point, then you have a choice. You said out loud you heard this. Then you have a choice as to whether or not you're going to choose to take action on that which you heard.

Jen: *I absolutely love this. It's so funny, we've never covered this before, have we? We haven't gotten to this piece. We've talked about hearing your guides. We've talked about creating. This is all about creating space and protecting but we've never said, "Say it out loud." Say it out loud. Say what you heard. I know I just cut you off so go ahead. Keep telling us what they're telling you. This is huge.*

Janelle: Sometimes, the other thing is it may be that you can't say it out loud. Say you're in a meeting at work or certain situations where you can't just go, "I'm feeling like I need to jump up and down," okay, probably not going to work.

You can write it down because that's another action that's validating what you hear. Sometimes when I'm teaching a class, it may not be appropriate for me to speak about what I'm hearing about for myself. I am at the point where I can just silently say, "Yes, I hear you, we'll adjust later." As long as you're taking the moment to acknowledge that which you feel and hear and are knowing within your being, your higher self with your Team will know that they can speak to you at any time. It creates the opening. It creates the vibration. Thus we're shifting your reality.

Jen: *When we started the conversation, too, you had said for a lot of us that don't always get quiet, you had said if you do it at the same time, your Team will show up for you at that time. But also it sounds like the more you acknowledge what you hear as you go through your day, the more you'll realize that they're constantly chattering inside of your head.*

Janelle: Right. Like in the case and point with the meeting, you might be in a business meeting. Your guides might pop in and say something to you about the meeting that maybe you need to speak about something else. That might lead to a doorway opening or it might prevent something else from occurring.

Jen: *Right, that you don't want, exactly.*

Janelle: Because I mean, they're seeing a world that your eyes will not adjust to yet because it exists all around you. We have trained ourselves not to see because really every child when they're young sees. That's why I was talking about the core that connects you. That's your innate natural state is to be able to see the other side clearly and hear them clearly, and feel them clearly. Everyone has that, everyone.

Jen: *It's amazing to me, Janelle, how many people don't believe that they do see. It is amazing to me how many people I come across, and they either say, "No, I don't have that," or "I don't have it as good as you have it."*

Janelle: True, I mean there are variations. Obviously there is variation. I mean, we're not all NFL players, right? There are people that are here to demonstrate the highest vehicle of what that is. Then there are some that have just come on the field, and they want to play in junior high. That's final. I came here to demonstrate that in all ways, shape, and forms. That's just what I'm here to do. Every ounce of my being, every cell of my being is programmed around demonstrating that full out in every single way. If I don't, then I have repercussions. Tests. Get your butt back in gear.

Jen: *Then they really turn up the volume, move it, move it.*

Janelle: I'm regular. I have fits and some points where I go like one day, it would be nice just to talk to someone and not hear additional conversation in my field. That would be great sometimes, or hear their own brain chatter. Sometimes that would be great, too.

Jen: *You would feel like you lost your hearing. "Steve, I've got to go check my hearing. Wait a minute." It would be all too quiet. I don't know if you would know what to do with yourself. You would be like, "Is this what you all hear every day, this?" Yes.*

Janelle: Yes, I mean, hearing the monotony of one hundred kazillion thoughts at any given moment, no. That's why I say it is so crowded, so—your body, as I experience people, there's so much mind drama going on. Then there's so much body drama going on. Your spirit is over there jumping through hoops going, "Hello, hello!" waving.

Jen: *We were here first, we were here first, hello at the end of the line.*

Janelle: They kind of flag you down the runway when you're doing whatever. Getting quiet for that ten minutes or whatever, or just acknowledging them in that moment that you felt something, "You know, I felt a nudge today," or confirmation.

They give you confirmation all the time. With us just the other day, we were having a conversation about something. They sent confirmation to me through someone else that didn't know we were having a conversation about that thing, but brought it through in conversation for me to validate that what you and I were sharing was in alignment with what they were wanting to create.

That was one of those things that if I hadn't been open to that phone call while I was standing there cooking dinner, I would have missed that message.

Jen: *Right, definitely. Again, for our listeners, it's all about first, getting quiet, right?*

Janelle: Yes, coming off that mind field.

Jen: *I want to throw out the listener line again. We have two people on hold right now but let me just throw out the lines in case anybody wants to call in with a question or for a reading. The listener line is 347-XXX-XXXX. It's* Spiritual Happy Hour *on Blog Talk Radio with Janelle Hoyland and Jen Louziotis.*

We're talking about hearing your guides, protecting your space, and getting clear with your vibrational output. Do you want to break for song, take the call, and then get on the flip side of the call, talk a little bit more about the vibrational output? What are you thinking?

Janelle: Yes, let's do that.

Jen: *A caller has a question about the veil. Is the veil lifting, are we multidimensional and what that means to us?*

Let me bring Michelle on. Hi Michelle, you're on the air with Janelle.

Caller #1: Hi, good morning. Hello ladies.

Janelle: Hi, how are you?

Caller #1: I'm great. How are you guys doing?

Janelle: Great, I'm glad you could join us. That's a beautiful question because really since I would say my mark would be 2000—well, we had a couple different places where the veil is thinner than it has been ever before.

Really, 2008 began a movement where we were no longer limited by something blocking us from seeing. Then we had more assistance. Ever since that mark, the veil between this side and that—and what she's talking about is spiritually, whenever I've connected in the past up until that point was kind of stepping through something or walking through something.

That's no longer my experience. Now it's just open field. In answering that question would be the veil, yes, is definitely lifted. That's the thing, too, is as we become closer to how we were

223

originally created, our original blueprint was to be able to see and feel, and experience heaven on earth.

That's what we're working with creating. We are at moments touching spaces of being, multidimensional beings. On different moments in time, there's opening for us to feel that sense of self that we're creating not just here but in other planes and other existences. The truth is we can affect our decisions that we make right now, affect both our past and our future at this very moment.

Jen: *Our past, too? Oh wow.*

Janelle: Yes, because we've been trained to understand that past lifetime, the term, means going backwards but in reality, they're all intermingled.

Jen: *Right.*

Caller #1: So if we're feeling like how most of us have been through trauma or just life itself, if we're healing those hurts, then kind of working them out, will we also be healing the past because I know future, I never heard about the past? I know the future, will be but will we be healing stuff from the past, too?

Janelle: Yes. That's why I say they're intermingled because when you make one decision, focus on an experience you had with your parents, let's say. Then you create a different vibrational field that wasn't available to you in your past.

So effectively your soul can choose a different choice.

Jen: *That's an awesome question, Michelle.*

Caller #1: *That's amazing.*

Janelle: Yes, it's way cool.

Jen: *Talk about your vibrational output, wow.*

Thank you. Janelle. Why now? Why is the veil so free now? Why 2008? Why then? Were we just not ready before? Or what, why?

Janelle: Here's the thing. We've come to this mark in the past where we tipped on the edge, and you've seen it. You heard it in different things like Atlantis, there's Lemuria, there's Mayan, there's all of these civilizations that were taken out for whatever reasons. They came to a certain point in their consciousness where they could no longer be. What for us is that we decided, "Okay, let's actually get it this time." We're presented with different opportunities for this to happen.

In the time when Jesus was alive, that was one of those opportunities when we could have shifted our total connection to divine and to our own innate abilities. Another time was then when Buddha was alive. Those are different moments in our soul's history where we've had these wonderful moments where the veil was lifted and you were able to take in really strong spiritual concepts and manifest them on this plane.

For whatever reason, it was not the right timing. We weren't ready, whatever the case may be but now, we actually are. It's been decreed that we've learned enough lifetimes. We've learned enough on a soul level that we can actually release our karma and choose to be not what our story is, that actually we are light beings. That has never been available to us.

Jen: *You were saying the other day, "No labels. Don't attach labels." I think that's kind of amazing for the vibrational push to be who you are, do what you are meant to do because you say this* *all the time, it's here and now. It's changing forwards, backwards. The present is just changing everything.*

Jump in and play. I think it's amazing because I think we say things over and over again in the show, but no show is ever the same. When it's presented another time, and saying, "Here it is," I just loved her question because it was so pertinent to today.

The veil is wide open, so here you go. You have it all. You know, you can listen, you can hear it. You can hear everything. WE do have it all. You've talked about us relating to each other Spirit to Spirit without labels. You tell us to drop the labels.

Janelle: For example: Because the rules are, if the label is parent, the child must be subservient to the parent and the parent knows more than the child, and all these other labels we put around that relationship that when you free up that space, you know, your child can then begin to learn from you. Then your child can actually teach you something about yourself.

Jen: *Right.*

Janelle: It's spirit to spirit. Then they can actually go and be effective people in the world, not moving from what the world is determining that they are but who they create their world to be.

Jen: *Yes, I really think we should do a whole show on that piece because, you know, they come in as teachers. We all come in as teachers but it gets so stifled, starting in kindergarten, first grade, second grade. Look up at the board and write this down, and do this, and do that.*

Janelle: Yes, all of the rules. I don't know if everyone knows this but I have a teenager and I have a thirteen-year-old, and then I have a two-and-a-half-year-old that's a boy. They're all very different beings. We have all different relationships.

They've taught me different things about myself. It's often with me as it is on the show, in my life, there's not like this separate conversation with my kids that I'm going to talk to you from spirit. They don't want to hear that usually.

You know, they get different... things will come out just in my everyday conversation that are messages delivered to my children from their guides, from their angels, from their Team that I have no control over at this point. That's just autopilot so it's just going to come out with them.

Some really astounding things that I've sat back and watched are delivered to these beautiful souls that have chosen me to be their mother in this life that it's really—they've got not an easy road in the sense of they're living with me every day. There's nothing that I don't know that goes on in their experience usually. They don't get away with much. They have different rules than other kids do. They have to be responsible for their vibrational output in the world. That's my requirement which I have taught them from day one. What is their belief system? We've talked about that.

You know, what do they believe in? What is their conviction? What are they here to demonstrate to the world from those belief systems? That's unique for each child. My oldest daughter doesn't have the same belief system as my middle daughter. My son definitely doesn't have the same belief system as my other two.

Jen: *Oh, we have to do a show on this. I'm telling you, you know me. It's huge.*

Janelle: I know that they didn't get the run-of-the-mill kind of mom in that sense but I'm extremely playful with them. We go outside and dance in the rain. We have pie fights. We just enjoy life. That's the one thing that I have demonstrated to them from when they were little is to really enjoy the experience of being connected to the earth and each other, and really expressing that. My oldest one still likes to dress up for Halloween. That's how my family is. That's truly the soul expressing itself. That was my highest desire, not just for my family but if I can do it with my family, then I can demonstrate it to everyone else because my family is energetically tied to me.

Jen: *Right.*

Janelle: If they're living authentically as children, what are they capable of as adults?

Jen: *Right, and never forgetting that, keep it fun, keep it going on, keep them connected. We have to do a show on this, Janelle. We have to, on I don't know what we're going to call it. I love the whole piece on belief system, figuring out what it is for each of your kids. It doesn't just, I think, obviously, just go for children. It goes for all of us to sort of think about it again ourselves as it's tied into our vibrational output.*

Janelle: I had to think about it again.

Jen: *That's just amazing. Do you want to sum it up for today? I can't believe we're once again over time.*

Janelle: Lightning speed, right?

Jen: *Yes.*

Show 11 – Fear and untruths we tell ourselves
Numerology perspective by Jen:
Life Path number 5

We ended with the vibration of freedom, adventure and fun in this show with Janelle reminding us again that our life is the playground meaning we can create anything and everything we want but we've got to be open to assistance from the other side.

CONCLUSION
LAST CALL—BEING, ALLOWING, DOING (B.A.D.)

Jen's moment of B.A.D

There's always a moment in each show when I let myself go completely—all my thoughts and fears about technical issues, or about how I am going to be perceived, or my own capabilities surrounding the show melt away. I just step in to the rhythm and flow of our creation that day. I literally forget that we are broadcasting live in front of an audience, and I let the Divine Conversation flow. It's my moment of being BAD, my moment of Being, Allowing and Doing at the same time. In that moment, I am just truly myself and I remember my part in all of this—my part in the Universe—my connection to God and everyone else in the world. The funny thing is that I'm floating on a higher vibration, feeling one hundred percent connected to everyone, led by God Himself while I'm talking to Janelle about how to solve problems in life. In order to reach that moment, I don't have to do anything special; I just have to be vulnerable enough to be myself.

Janelle's moment of B.A.D.

So this is for me more about understanding what I am in reflection to my external world. I had issues for such a long time, feeling as if I needed to restrain myself. My whole life has been about how I feel around others. It never occurred to me to think about how they felt around me. That gave me the Being part. Being present to what was occurring through conversation and interaction. I needed to learn how to allow things to unfold. You see, I became a master at fixing, altering and shifting. So much that this caused me to really allow people around me to Be as well. In this way, I allowed the universe to take the wheel. After all, they know a better, faster route then the one I would take. It may make me uncomfortable, but I am present. Doing is the part I do best. I have always been a get-it-done kind of person. What I have allowed is it is better to have a Team to accomplish big goals. I would suggest you find your own moments of B.A.D.

Last call by Jen

May, 2014—some random Monday—it hit me as I was running up the stairs of our basement. Midway up the first flight I stopped dead in my tracks and literally said out loud, "OH MY GOD." I had just finished cleaning up the toys in the basement playroom and getting the room ready because Janelle was coming for a visit. She was coming to hang out with me for a few days and during that time she was going to see some clients at my house and teach a class in my basement. Halfway up the stairs, I thought to myself, "Okay, the basement is all ready for Janelle to teach," and that's when it hit me. I really had forgotten about that tantrum of a prayer I had put out to God in 1997, but saying out loud the phrase, "Teaching classes in my basement" brought it back to me.

I had a flash of my apartment in New York City, my feeling of frustration and anger and the feeling of being at my wit's end. I stood there for a few minutes feeling humbled and extremely grateful at the same time. It took a few minutes for the magnitude of what I had been given over the last several years to sink in. As I stood there in the middle of the steps, I listed everything I had asked for in that prayer and checked off all that had been answered and all the ways my life had profoundly changed.

- I had asked for an intuitive psychic healer (before they were famous) to come into my life and teach me in person.
- I asked for that person to demonstrate how to hear and connect to Divine Guidance.
- I asked for that person to answer my personal questions and give me feedback.
- I asked for a road map to solve problems so I could live a better life—a cheat sheet of sorts—that would break down solutions into smaller steps so I could better understand how to solve problems in my life and learn to connect to my guides.
- I wanted to be taught on a regular basis—weekly is what I had in mind.
- Finally, I asked that same psychic healer teach classes in my basement.

God listened to every word and answered every piece of my prayer right down to the last detail of showing me that he knew I was holding on to Sonia's book when I was freaking out about my life and asking for help and even the detail of teaching classes in my basement, which I don't even think I meant at the time but He threw that in for fun. He had always been there, knew everything I was experiencing and because I wasn't able to hear all the messages he was already sending me, he sent Janelle to me to show me through demonstration how to connect to the Divine and how to move through the more challenging parts of life and do it in a way that was fun.

When I look back at my original prayer, I see that I just asked for the end result to happen. I focused on getting connected and finding solutions to my problems. I had no vision for how this was going to occur in my life—I just wanted my problems to go away. As I partnered with Janelle week by week to create *Spiritual Happy Hour*, I went through many emotional ups and downs and put up a ton of roadblocks in my own learning, but I was always met with unconditional love, joy, support, strength, guidance, patience, humor, laughter, and celebration during every single show and in our friendship. I wasn't expecting any of that when I asked for help.

Janelle was ready and willing to dive deep into every topic we chose together and she held my hand as I navigated new waters and learned a new way of being in the world. While I approached many of our shows "kicking and screaming" about the technical/computer production aspect, I opened myself up completely to the process of really being led by God. For me that meant going inward and really taking an honest—and sometimes painful—look at the way I lived my life, and becoming open and willing to change. Through this process, I learned how to finally be true to who I am and to create from that place of authenticity.

If this can happen to me when I wasn't paying attention, wasn't putting my real faith in God and even forgot about what I had asked for in the first place, then anything you dream for yourself can happen for you, too. You are loved and supported in everything you do in this lifetime and beyond; in everything you do and in all moments of your life.

Guidance really is one long flowing conversation between you and God and your Team. I was transformed by the information brought through Janelle on our show and I hope that you are as well. Thank you for being a part of this journey and sharing *Spiritual Happy Hour* with us.

Last call by Janelle

Putting a conclusion on this book is like that great lunch with girlfriends or a funny movie that made you laugh so hard you don't want it to end. You see for me it's finally having someone ask the right questions in a way everyone can understand. This caused me so much relief I don't have words. Honestly, my Team and I view this book and the radio show as the universe's way of letting you have inside information in a clear precise way. The purpose is to help you more in integrating things as a daily experience. As I write this section, tears rolling down my face, I have no words to say to come close to how I feel in letting this piece of my journey be totally free for all of you. My intimacy, vulnerability, and process is something I had held very privately. I know that as you read each section, you will learn more about yourself as both Jen and I did being in it together.

I walked through many of my own lessons in this journey with Jen. Some of those included learning how to really trust in another person. I also allowed myself to be seen instead of standing in the back like no one saw me anyhow (insert laughter). This is the beginning and an ending for me. I am stepping into a new way of being while letting my Team lead me even further inward. Honestly, I feel totally naked. I am great with that raw presence of being free. I pushed myself through so many roadblocks getting this done. It's like I climbed a mountain. My knees are raw and my feet blistered. I have no more room for anything less to be delivered through me in this project.

Please know that every word written here is backed by a profound intention shared by me and my Team to transform the way you partner with the universe (your Team). Knowing this, I have left nothing on the table. I went full out all the way. This is not in the eyes of perfection but through the eyes of I know what you have asked for both conscious and unconsciously. Allow this to move you as it did me in so many ways. What we have created for you is a blueprint, a real life walking demonstration of communication, trust, friendship and intuition. Please do reread it; different phrases will come through that you did not see before. Thank you for stepping into our *Spiritual Happy Hour*.

JENNIFER LOUZIOTIS

At the age five Jennifer Louziotis began to question her place and purpose in the world and the Universe. She soon became determined to learn how to hone her intuition to connect to the spirit world. She studied many psychic and intuitive teachers but was lead to Janelle Hoyland via Divine Appointment. As the co-creator and co-host of *Spiritual Happy Hour* Radio Show, Jennifer uses her intuition to ask interview question and with Janelle Hoyland is able to take tangible and intangible spiritual concepts and transform them into practical application for the masses. It is her joy and passion to share this information with the world.

She received a Master's Degree in Social Work Administration from Columbia University School of Social Work. She is a certified Intuitive Career, Relationship and Grief coach.

When she is not on air asking Janelle questions she can be found playing with her 2 children or hanging out with her husband of 12 years in New Jersey.

www.spiritualhappyhour.com

REV. JANELLE HOYLAND, PH.D.

 Rev. Janelle Hoyland, PH.D. is a renowned soul pathway healer, divine psychic, a transformation specialist, a lover of life to its fullest, and a face your fears dead on person. She has done numerous radio shows and speaking engagements. Since the age of 19 she has been seeing clients from all over the world.

Janelle's life has been filled with challenges and gifts just like anyone else. She was born aware of her connection to the universe knowing and hearing her own loving guidance never leaving her side. She has been taught by the universe to shift your awareness. She goes into the blueprint of each soul to plunge out your soul system from debris while giving you a life line to your soul path direction. It is a makeover for your soul.

Currently she lives with her husband of 19 years and 3 wonderful kids in Texas.

www.janellehoyland.com